内容

Introduction	2
Prologue	4
Chapter 1　Why we should amend constitution now ?	10
Chapter 2　Constitution Art.9 and Self-Defence Force	22
Chapter 3　Emperor: Symbol of Japan	37
Chapter 4　Necessity to change Article 9	40
Chapter 5　National Defense and the Japan-US Security Treaty	48
Chapter 6　About the Collective Defense Right	54
Epilogue – In Search of World Eternal Peace	84
Afterword	91
References and Bibliography	92

Introduction

Why wars happen?

War in which people kill each other ········ every one wishes for a peaceful world without war.

Nevertheless, why wars happen?
Can't we get rid of war?

Many people may think "As long as human beings are alive, struggles never end. Such a thing is impossible." But please do not give up. In fact, Japan has not been involved in war for more than 70 years after World War II, and almost all Japanese people after my generation are going to fulfil their lives without any experience of war.

War cannot be eliminated only by just shouting out "No more war!!"
But if every one of you who reads this book acts by thinking in your own head with firm belief never to engage in any war, it will be possible to let your descendant avoid war.

Why should we amend Constitution Art.9? —— preparing for the plebiscite

In the last world war, Japan brought great damages to neighboring countries as well as her people themselves experienced various horrors including the world's only atomic bomb damages. From that experience, Japanese people learned lessons that at the dispute among nations one should not intimidate the opponent by force of arms or use the force to the opponent as purpose to compel one's own position to the other, and thus they created Article 9.

Constitution Art.9 determined the eternal renunciation of the use of force as means of settling international disputes, and on the top of it the world-leading army renunciation clause was created. The provisions to waiver wars of aggression are employed by many nations in the world, but they seldom went to such renunciation of military forces as was employed in Japan.

For 70 years after World War II, the big five victory as well as other nations have been continuing war everywhere in the world by way of protecting own nationals and national interests.   Meanwhile Japan, under this Constitution Art.9, neither joined in any wars in the world nor oppressed any anti-governmental movement or demonstration by using her JSDF (Japan Self-Defense Force).   With duty of protecting one of world's leading GNP power as well as country's long coastline JSDF keeps appropriate forces against troops of surrounding military powers but the characteristics of JSDF are completely different from those of military forces of other nations.

Now in Japan, by using phrases like "imposed constitution", "JSDF is obviously military force", etc. commentary of which is quite easy to people's ears, the movement towards the constitutional revision is growing.

Present Prime Minister Shinzo Abe firmly believes that the revision of Art. 9 is paramount for keeping our nation peace. Although the twists and turns may come for a few years, the national referendum should be conducted in the end as the popularity of Shinzo Abe presumably would continue for several years.

Is the amendment to Art.9 necessary to defend the peace and security of the country?

I hope that people who have taken up this book will go to vote at the plebiscite, being confident in Japan's post-war history and being proud of the constitution they themselves have, and that Japan will continue to enjoy peaceful and affluent society so as to contribute to the world peace.

I shall be very happy if the readers of this booklet will get some hints to understand more correctly the meaning of Japanese Constitution Art.9.

Prologue

In April 2001, Prime Minister Junichiro Koizumi, who achieved highest start of inauguration with the approval rating 80% in opinion polls, cast a stone to the public immediately after the formation of the cabinet by putting such an easy-to-understand phrase as "It is quite unnatural to say that JSDF is not a military force".

Since then the conservative lawmakers again began to speak loudly the constitutional revision, and in 2012 the re-elected Prime Minister Shinzo Abe started to expedite the movement towards the constitutional revision centering on Art.9, in conformity with the wishes of his grandfather Nobusuke Kishi (37th Prime Minister and war-time Munitions Minister), backed by the experience of his first cabinet and by the overwhelming people's support to his national economic policy.

When we argue on revision of the constitution, there are many points and issues, i.e. which part or which article must be amended. But in any case, we must avoid the argument based on the emotional and/or affective thinking. At the plebiscite, we should not say "Yes" or "No" urged just by our mood or feeling.

Whether a text of a law is inadequate and must be revised or not should be judged after you finish reading the text. According to the Asahi Shimbun (p5 of May 2, 2001), even some of the intellectuals who were invited to attend the Constitution Research Committee of the Diet had not earnestly read the text before. Then how many citizens in general have actually read the text of the constitution?

It may be a matter of course that we do not read in earnest such tiresome sentences as legal provisions. However, it is necessary to read at least the controversial Article 9, because it contains the problem pertaining to the survival of every one of our nationals. Here we should like to focus on Article 9, and consider whether or not it is really necessary to revise this provision.

Let us read Article 9 of Japanese Constitution

The Constitution of Japan
Promulgated on November 3, 1946
Came into effect on May 3, 1947

CHAPTER II

RENUNCIATION OF WAR

Article 9.
　Aspiring sincerely to an international peace based on justice and order, the Japanese people forever renounce war as a sovereign right of the nation and the threat or use of force as means of settling international disputes.
　In order to accomplish the aim of the preceding paragraph, land, sea, and air forces, as well as other war potential, will never be maintained. The right of belligerency of the state will not be recognized.

　This provision follows "Preamble" and "Chapter I Emperor", and consists of one chapter and one article as Art.9.

　Let us read the first paragraph.
　It is determined clearly that the Japanese people "forever renounce war" "and the threat or use of force as means of settling international disputes."

　The top phrase, "Aspiring sincerely to an international peace based on justice and order, " shows the motivation to this article and together with the other phrase, "as a sovereign right of the nation",　are the modifiers to reinforce the expression of the principle.

　Thus, getting rid of the rhetoric, it becomes very clear that this first paragraph means that when Japan is caught in any international conflict, she never starts war with other party, never threats the other by her forces, and/or never actually uses them for its settlement.   That is to say, she is determined to resolve all disputes by discussions (i.e. diplomatic negotiations) and not by using armed forces.

  Let us read the second paragraph.
  In order to actually realize the principle of renunciation of war as means of settling international disputes as determined in first paragraph, it is declared clearly that they do not maintain armed forces and any other war potential, and on the top of it they denied the so-called "right of belligerency of the state".

  To ensure more completely the principle expressed in the first paragraph, this second paragraph defines that they do not have any armed forces that are mobilized simply by order of political power --- this provision is unprecedented and unique in the world.
  Under the provision, no armed forces exist in Japan as long as this constitution keep effect.

    As you see, two paragraphs of this article are both quite explicit, and every citizen easily understand the meaning when they read the sentence without objecting.   At least there is no room to say that the sentences are unclear or ambiguous.

Background of the provision

  Every legal provision has its proper purpose.   Now for what purpose this article was made?

  The constitution was promulgated on November 3, 1946, a year and two months later than August 15, 1945, the date of Japan's literally devastating defeat of the War.

  Japan, for the four years before war-end plus previous tens of years, has converged the public opinion towards the alliance with Germany and Italy against US-Britain-France-Dutch coalition hand in hand with the Asian and Chinese political leaders bearing the same vision.

Most Japanese people were determined to win the Greater East Asian War with patriotic spirit to sacrifice family and social life as urged by the powers (government) in order to realize the international justice that the Emperor longed for.

Up until the last day of defeat the Japanese nationals had exerted their utmost effort to defend their homeland in vain. And, at the time when they failed to defend their nation and the country was occupied by the enemy, they realized that such predicted and dreadful situation as their wives and children are to be humiliated by the enemy did not come. On the contrary, the fact that they could not protect the nation brought them a peaceful daily life again to their relief.

The citizens thought over for the first time how they should protect their own lives when the state (including, politicians, bureaucrats, academics, the media and any others with powers) guided them wrong. It can be implied that such a consensus of the people in general was summarized in the Constitution Article 9.

Who addresses this provision? To whom?

This provision is understood without objecting in such a way as the nationals, through their experience of their history till the war-defeat, intended to put a restriction to the movement of the State powers.

The characteristics of wars and/or armed forces are such that the State power makes it legal by force for some of the nationals to commit illegal acts. Wars justify the acts of the State to kill human beings, to take out other's property, the freedom of occupation choice, the freedom of assembly, association and expression, the freedom of religion, the fundamental right of labor, the academic freedom, etc., all of which should be inviolable.

The conflicts between nations are all conflicts of justice vs. justice as is obvious in history. The World War II was, for Japanese people, a sacred war against devilish US-Britain who destruct world peace, and, for US-Britain-France-Dutch, it was a war against world-enemy fascistic alliance of Japan-Germany-Italy. In the middle-east wars, for Iran, U.S. are the incarnation of imperialism and those Arabic nations on US side are the nations where a few ruling people dominate the country and are enemies of the poor Iraqi citizens. But on the other hand, for the United States, those Hussain factions are tyrannies who trample on the well-being of the people of Iraq and must be eliminated as soon as possible for the peace of the entire world.

It goes without saying that there exist diplomatic negotiations to resolve international disputes. However, it is not secured whether the negotiations always end amicably. The negotiations often get entangled and the disputes are not resolved. In such moment, a nation having power tends to use it so as to compel her position to the other, which has been quite usual in human history. Therefore, now ordinary countries in the world admit the exercise of war as a means of solving international disputes. Right now, the strongest Power, United States moves to correct the international injustice by use and/or threat of force, and even by war, the principles of which have been supported by her nationals.

That the State solves the dispute by force specifically means that the State orders by using her supreme power for her own nationals to kill other nationals. That is to say, most countries in the world, in such cases as other nations do not agree to a country's position and as the other country's position is judged to be injustice in her own view, then as a means to change that other nation's unreasonable position, order to her nationals to go to kill other nationals systematically as a matter of emergency. At present, many people support this viewpoint.

Japanese people fought in the World War II to defend the nation, but the defeat changed the interpretation over nightly. It became to be a war of invasion. The leaders were sentenced to death and many others were punished.　People had to live their lives with agony.

　They reached to work out the way not to be pushed to war in the name of patriotism or any other eloquent slogans. That is, they force the government renounce war as means to settle the international disputes and they take out from the State the right of belligerency which compels them to kill others.　The people determined that principle in the constitution which the government must obey.　Furthermore, in order to ensure that restriction to the government, they added the second paragraph to let her not keep any armed forces.
Thus, the Japanese Constitution Article 9.

　This Article was created by the people on purpose to defend themselves from the State so as not to be ordered to go to war on the pretext of justice or national interest.

http://japan.kantei.go.jp/constitution_and_government_of_japan/constitution_e.html

Chapter 1 Why we should amend constitution now ?

1." Forced constituion" is not true

Q1.
 In order to achieve real independence of Japan, should we not amend the present constitution which powerless Japan was forced to accept by General Douglas MacArthur under the post-war occupation?

A1.

 As the phrase "Constitution was forced for Japan to accept under GHQ(=Allied Headquarters of the Supreme Commander for the Allied Powers)" is simple in logic and easy to understand, I am afraid that young people, who do not try to know well the then situation and the actual process of the establishment of the present constitution, tend to be pulled in biased direction.

 Immediately after the war-end and in the very chaotic society in Japan, a variety of people such as private sector, academia, media, governmental organizations, etc. presented the draft of new constitution.　National debate was boiling concerning the various proposals.　Among them are those from leftist communist party which aim for labors' one-party rule to rightist national polity worshipers who long for maintaining unbroken line of Emperors.

 Under these circumstances, the Japanese Government together with GHQ exerted the utmost efforts to make up a unified governmental plan.　However the negotiation, between GHQ,who wished to introduce democracy in more complete form and government who wanted the Emperor monarchy to remain in as stronger degree as possible, was very hard.

 Whether to pursue the Emperor as a war criminal was another serious problem. In final stage, in order to survive Emperor system under the sovereignty of people both agreed to the idea of "symbol Emperor", and as a result of the deliberations in both houses of the Imperial legislature, the Japanese Constitution together with the so-called post-war democracy was finally born. I hope that young people will listed to the voices of the generations who know this history through experience.

(from Asahi Shimbun "KOE(Voices)" 2013 / 5 / 27 Kato Yasuya, 76 -year-old, Retired)

Concerning the constitutional revision, wide range of people from left-wing communist or trade union, scholars relating to those organizations, left-wing scholars representing Morito Tatsuo, newspapers, other media, to private proclaimed constitutional researchers, mainstream scholars like Sasaki Soichi(Kyoto Univ.),Minobe Tatsukichi(Tokyo Univ.) as well as long-time constitutional scholars like Suzuki Yasuzo, announced their proposals and/or ideas, which led to the nation-wide discussion.

The cabinet of Shidehara Kijuro appointed commercial law scholar Matsumoto Joji (Prof.of Tokyo Univ.) as the Minister in charge of Constitution and worked hard to establish the unified government draft of the constitution in cooperation with GHQ, who was the supreme authority of Japan under occupation.

While GHQ wished to introduce democracy to as much extent as possible, the government intended to maintain Japan's historic "national polity" which they presented at the time of acceptance of the Potsdam Declaration as an unyielding condition. It might be a matter of course that even such a top-class intellectual as Prof. Matsumoto could not change their mind to democracy so quickly, as they had been in the middle of imperialism just until a few months before. Therefore it might be also quite natural that GHQ was astonished to read Feb.1946 Mainichi daily newspaper scoop revealing the"Private Draft of Government Constitutional Problem Investigation Committee", the contents of which were still on the Emperor sovereignty principles and the draft was a mere partly revision of Meiji Constitution.

The private draft which Matsumoto Joji presented contained "Article 3. The Emperor is sacred and inviolable.", "Article 11. The Emperor has the supreme command of the Army and Navy.",etc.. and those were based on the monarchy sovereignty principles and virtually a revised version of the Meiji Constitution. The then Japanese rulers did not think yet that the nationals would welcome the democracy.

Rather GHQ was agnostic about the past history and understood the feelings of the Japanese people after World War II from a totally different perspective. Finally, GHQ proposed to the government to publicize both the government draft and the GHQ draft together.   The cabinet feared that in that case his mandate would become unsustainable and so he finally decided to accept the idea of GHQ draft.

Among the allied nations (specifically "Allied Council for Japan") led by US, there existed a strong opinion from Soviet Union, Australia, etc. to suit the Emperor as a war criminal and those believed that without eliminating Emperor system Japanese militarism should come back again.   However, GHQ, who was actually to be engaged in the occupation, was fully aware of the Japanese people's strong respect for the Emperor, and so he opposed to the indictment of the Emperor.   He firmly believed that to carry out the occupation, they should keep the Emperor in some way or other for the country's stability.

GHQ on one hand firmly insisted his intention to introduce democracy against the Japanese government's draft based on historic national polity, and on the other agreed to keep Emperor under "the principles of national sovereignty" as "symbol of national unity "so that the Emperor's authority was very much limited. Emphasizing such completed Constitution of democracy and the Emperor symbol, the United States could fend off the requests of the Soviet Union, etc. and at the same time, the GHQ was able to carry out occupation successfully.

It may be true that from the viewpoint of the then Japanese power (governing people) they were forced to accept the "democracy" by MacArthur.

However, if GHQ had not intervened at that stage, in other words if GHQ had not put his opinion in the process, the Japanese constitution would have been adopted in line of the draft of Constitutional Problem Investigation Committee (so called, Matsumoto draft) and the "post war democracy" of Japan should not have been realized.

Actual Title of Source	Kenpo Kaisei Shian Genko
Date	[January 4, 1946]
Document Number	
Repository (reproduction)	
Repository	Matsumoto Papers, Legal History Section, Faculty of Law, University of Tokyo
Note	

"Forced constitution" argument cannot be the reason for the revision of the constitution which opened way to introduce "national sovereignty" and "pacifism" earnestly welcomed by the majority of nationals.

Source: "Birth of the Constitution of Japan" National Diet Library (http://www.ndl.go.jp/constitution/e/shiryo/01shiryo.html)

2-8 Joji Matsumoto, "Draft of Tentative Revision of the Constitution Draft"

This is the Tentative Revision of the Constitution that Matsumoto submitted to the 10th examination meeting (subcommittee meeting) of the Constitutional Problems Investigation Committee on January 9, 1946, and its draft written in his own hand. Matsumoto, who had declared that he would take the initiative in formulating a draft proposal after the sixth general meeting of the committee on December 26, drafted the

Actual Title of Source	Kenpo Kaisei Shian (Ichigatsu Yokka Ko) Matsumoto Joji
Date	January 4, 1946
Document Number	Irie Toshio Papers: 9
Repository (reproduction)	
Repository	National Diet Library
Note	

reformation proposal during the New Year's Holiday and completed it on January 4, 1946. He presented this proposal as the basis of his report on the constitutional reform problem to the Emperor on January 7.

Then on the 9th, it was distributed at the 10th examination meeting of the Investigation Committee, but was withdrawn after the meeting. On the 12th at the 11th examination meeting, Matsumoto made amendments to the proposal responding to most of the criticism made during the previous meeting.

- Preview[Kenpo Kaisei Shian Genko]
- Larger[Kenpo Kaisei Shian Genko]

10.5 ポ、43 字×34 行（設六判 43 字×17 行/頁の 2 頁分）

- Preview[Kenpo Kaisei Shian (Ichigatsu Yokka Ko) Matsumoto Joji]
- Larger[Kenpo Kaisei Shian (Ichigatsu Yokka Ko) Matsumoto Joji]

(http://www.ndl.go.jp/constitution/index.html) 国立国会図書館「日本国憲法の誕生」)

憲法改正要綱（松本案）1946 年 2 月 8 日

第一章　天皇
一　第三条ニ「天皇ハ神聖ニシテ侵スヘカラス」トアルヲ「天皇ハ至尊ニシテ侵スヘカラス」ト改ムルコト
二　第七条所定ノ衆議院ノ解散ハ同一事由ニ基ツキ之ヲ命スルコトヲ得サルモノトスルコト
三　第八条所定ノ緊急勅令ヲ発スルニハ議院法ノ定ムル所ニ依リ帝国議会常置委員ノ諮詢ヲ経ルヲ要スルモノトスルコト
四　第九条中ニ「公共ノ安寧秩序ヲ保持シ及臣民ノ幸福ヲ増進スル為ニ必要ナル命令」トアルヲ「行政ノ目的ヲ達スル為ニ必要ナル命令」ト改ムルコト（要綱十参照）
五　第十一条中ニ「陸海軍」トアルヲ「軍」ト改メ且第十二条ノ規定ヲ改メ編制及常備兵額ハ法律ヲ以テ之ヲ定ムルモノトスルコト（要綱二十参照）
六　第十三条ノ規定ヲ改メ戦ヲ宣シ和ヲ議シ又ハ法律ヲ以テ定ムルヲ要スル事項ニ関ル条約若ハ二重大ナル義務ヲ負ハシムル条約ヲ締結スルニハ帝国議会ノ協賛ヲ経ルヲ要スルモノトスルコト但シ内外ノ情形ニ因リ帝国議会ノ召集ヲ待ツコト能ハサル緊急ノ必要アルトキハ帝国議会常置委員ノ諮詢ヲ経ルヲ以テ足ルモノトシ此ノ場合ニ於テハ次ノ会期ニ於テ帝国議会ニ報告シ其ノ承諾ヲ求ムヘキモノトスルコト
七　第十五条ニ「天皇ハ爵位勲章及其ノ他ノ栄典ヲ授与ス」トアルヲ「天皇ハ栄典ヲ授与ス」ト改ムルコト
第二章　臣民権利義務

15

八　第二十条中ニ「兵役ノ義務」トアルヲ「公益ノ為必要ナル役務ニ服スル義務」ト改ムルコト

九　第二十八条ノ規定ヲ改メ日本臣民ハ安寧秩序ヲ妨ケサル限ニ於テ信教ノ自由ヲ有スルモノトスルコト

十　日本臣民ハ本章各条ニ掲ケタル場合ノ外凡テ法律ニ依ルニ非スシテ其ノ自由及権利ヲ侵サルルコトナキ旨ノ規定ヲ設クルコト

十一　非常大権ニ関スル第三十一条ノ規定ヲ削除スルコト

十二　軍人ノ特例ニ関スル第三十二条ノ規定ヲ削除スルコト

第三章　帝国議会

十三　第三十三条以下ニ「貴族院」トアルヲ「参議院」ト改ムルコト

十四　第三十四条ノ規定ヲ改メ参議院ハ参議院法ノ定ムル所ニ依ル選挙又ハ勅任セラレタル議員ヲ以テ組織スルモノトスルコト

十五　衆議院ニ於テ引続キ三回其ノ総員三分ノ二以上ノ多数ヲ以テ可決シテ参議院ニ移シタル法律案ハ参議院ノ議決アルト否トヲ問ハス帝国議会ノ協賛ヲ経タルモノトスル旨ノ規定ヲ設クルコト

十六　第四十二条所定ノ帝国議会ノ会期「三箇月」ヲ改メ「三箇月以上ニ於テ議院法ノ定メタル期間」トスルコト

十七　第四十五条所定ノ衆議院解散後ニ於ケル帝国議会ヲ召集スヘキ期限「五箇月以内」ヲ「三箇月以内」ト改ムルコト

十八　第四十八条但書ノ規定ヲ改メ両議院ノ会議ヲ秘密会ト為スハ専ラ其ノ院ノ決議ニ依ルモノトスルコト

十九　会期前ニ逮捕セラレタル議員ハ其ノ院ノ要求アルトキハ会期中之ヲ釈放スヘキ旨ノ規定ヲ設クルコト

第四章　国務大臣及枢密顧問

二十　第五十五条第一項ノ規定ヲ改メ国務各大臣ハ天皇ヲ輔弼シ帝国議会ニ対シテ其ノ責ニ任スルモノトシ且軍ノ統帥ニ付亦同シキ旨ヲ明記スルコト

二十一　衆議院ニ於テ国務各大臣ニ対スル不信任ヲ議決シタルトキハ解散アリタル場合ヲ除ク外其ノ職ニ留ルコトヲ得サル旨ノ規定ヲ設クルコト(要綱二参照)

二十二　国務各大臣ヲ以テ内閣ヲ組織スル旨及内閣ノ官制ハ法律ヲ以テ之ヲ定ムル旨ノ規定ヲ設クルコト

二十三　枢密院ノ官制ハ法律ヲ以テ之ヲ定ムル旨ノ規定ヲ設クルコト

第五章　司法

二十四　第六十一条ノ規定ヲ改メ行政事件ニ関ル訴訟ハ別ニ法律ノ定ムル所ニ依リ司法裁判所ノ管轄ニ属スルモノトスル

第六章　会計
二十五　参議院ハ衆議院ノ議決シタル予算ニ付増額ノ修正ヲ為スコトヲ得サル旨ノ規定ヲ設クルコト
二十六　第六十六条ノ規定ヲ改メ皇室経費中其ノ内廷ノ経費ニ限リ定額ニ依リ毎年国庫ヨリ之ヲ支出シ増額ヲ要スル場合ヲ除ク外帝国議会ノ協賛ヲ要セサルモノトスルコト
二十七　第六十七条ノ規定ヲ改メ憲法上ノ大権ニ基ツケル既定ノ歳出ハ政府ノ同意ナクシテ帝国議会之ヲ廃除シ又ハ削減スルコトヲ得ルモノトスルコト
二十八　予備費ヲ以テ予算ノ外ニ生シタル必要ノ費用ニ充ツルトキ及予備費外ニ於テ避クヘカラサル予算ノ不足ヲ補フ為ニ又ハ予算ノ外ニ生シタル必要ノ費用ニ充ツル為ニ支出ヲ為ストキハ帝国議会常置委員ノ諮詢ヲ経ヘキ旨ノ規定ヲ設クルコト
二十九　第七十条所定ノ財政上ノ緊急処分ヲ為スニハ帝国議会常置委員ノ諮詢ヲ経ルヲ要スルモノトスルコト
三十　第七十一条ノ規定ヲ改メ予算不成立ノ場合ニハ政府ハ会計法ノ定ムル所ニ依リ暫定予算ヲ作成シ予算成立ニ至ルマテノ間之ヲ施行スヘキモノトシ此ノ場合ニ於テ帝国議会閉会中ナルトキハ速ニ之ヲ召集シ其ノ年度ノ予算ト共ニ暫定予算ヲ提出シ其ノ承諾ヲ求ムルヲ要スルモノトスルコト

第七章　補則
三十一　両議院ノ議員ハ各々其ノ院ノ総員二分ノ一以上ノ賛成ヲ得テ憲法改正ノ議案ヲ発議スルコトヲ得ル旨ノ規定ヲ設クルコト
三十二　天皇ハ帝国議会ノ議決シタル憲法改正ヲ裁可シ其ノ公布及執行ヲ命スル旨ノ規定ヲ設クルコト
三十三　憲法及皇室典範変更ノ制限ニ関スル第七十五条ノ規定ヲ削除スルコト
三十四　以上憲法改正ノ各規定ノ施行ニ関シ必要ナル規定ヲ設クルコト

出所：日本国憲法の誕生（国会図書館資料）
http://www.ndl.go.jp/constitution/shiryo/03shiryo.html

2. Contents are more important than process

Q2.
 We Japanese cannot accept the constitution influenced by GHQ under occupation. We must abolish the present constitution which was strongly influenced by thoughts of the United States.

A2.
 Certainly, the people in power in the Japanese government at the time of drafting the constitution lacked in the deliberation in reasoning why the war started and why Japanese people had to experience such tragedy and in working out the way how to let the people escape from any more wars.   They were simply ignorant of understanding the atmosphere of the people in general.

 Abolishment of armed forces was initially proposed by Shidehara Kijuro. Douglas MacArthur wrote in his memoir that he was astonished to hear this proposal from Shidehara.   Apart from who first created this principle, the imperial diet adopted the constitution, of which Article 9 clearly specified that the country should not maintain armed forces and accumulated the peaceful history of more than 70 years.   When we discuss whether we were forced to accept GHQ draft or not, the argument should be pointed on "National Sovereignty" or "Imperial Monarchy" and not on "abolishment of armed forces".

 It cannot be the reason for constitutional revision that the idea of foreign people was reflected to the enactment of the constitution.   The historic 17-article-constitution of Shotoku Taishi, that is supposed to be the oldest constitution in Japan (although the regulation bears the word constitution, its characteristics are completely different from that of the modern constitution putting frame in the political action of the government power. This "constitution" mainly defines the acting principles of the officials.) was strongly influenced by the philosophy of then China (Sui dynasty).   Japan's first modern constitution, Imperial Constitution of Japan, was strongly affected by the thinking of then Germany (Prussia) and other Western nations.   Especially its Article 3, i.e. " The Emperor is sacred and inviolable", was born with the strong guidance of German advisor Hermann Roesler.

It is all right to refer to the legislative process when interpreting the constitution, law and/or regulation, the most important is the contents of the finished law, and so it does not make sense to claim the constitutional reform by reason of the process of legislature.

If the people's majority long for the change from the national sovereignty to the Emperor monarchy and/or want for having the armed forces as other nations have, it is quite all right to go to the constitutional revision. However it is quite questionable to go to the constitutional revision by reason of foreign influence without discussing the contents of the constitution that has been established in the society during more than 70 after the war.

3. The change of times cannot be the reason for the constitutional revision.

Q3.

More than 70 years have passed since the constitution was enacted and the era is now totally different. Should we not keep such an old-fashioned constitution anymore and adopt a new one which is suitable to modern age ?

A3.

Of course any rules of the society should be changed flexibly according to the change of the times. In monarchy the monarch changes the law taking in the opinions of the chief retainers, and in democracy people change the law in national gathering of representatives of their own, i.e. the parliament.

In this case, in order that the monarch or the parliament does not make up extreme legal changes by the momentum of the era, the modern constitution is established to previously stipulate the foremost rules on basic matters to suppress the runaway of the monarch and/or the parliament.

Japanese Constitution stipulates in its Article 41 "The Diet shall be the highest organ of state power, and shall be the sole law-making organ of the State."

If the law is not suitable or is not adequate to the present age, the Diet, which is the assembly of people's representative, has the duty to revise the law to make it appropriate.

And, when it becomes clear that the Diet cannot change the law or establish the new law because of the regulation of the Constitution, then the constitutional revision becomes necessary. Amendments to the Constitution are to be initiated by the Diet through a concurring vote of 2/3 or more of all the members of each House and shall be submitted to the people for ratification, which shall require the affirmative vote of a majority of all votes cast thereon.

So, the Constitution can be amended at any time. If you have a text by which the Diet cannot establish laws which they believe are necessary for people's happiness, such a text must be amended. However, the idea of change somewhere because of the lapse of time without discussing which contents of the text are inappropriate, of the constitution that has been played its role perfectly for more than a half century, is hard to understand.

If a law does meet the present society, the Diet should change the law duly. If the Constitution is an obstacle to change laws, the necessity of the law should be discussed first.

Chapter 2 Constitution Art.9 and Self-Defence Force

4. It is not necessary to put defense right in the Constitution

Q4.

You should defend your own country by yourself. Under the current Constitution Japan cannot keep her security by depending on the shoulder and piggyback of the United States indefinitely. To deal with Chinese maritime expansion, the nuclear attack threat from North Korea, the stubborn attitude of Russia over the northern territory, etc., it is quite essential that the peace-addicted Japan should amend her Constitution so as to cope with those hostile countries by her own military forces. Japan should amend her Constitution Article 9 and specify clearly her right of self-defense.

A4.

"Defend your country by yourself" --- it is surely right.
Japan has exactly kept her security by herself for the past 70 years after the war. It is our hope that our descendants will keep on securing country's safety and peace forever.

The Constitution does not have the provision of self-defense right. It is a matter of course that a nation defends her existence by herself, whether or not the constitution specifies its right explicitly.

Any creature protects his body from others who try to harm him. Cats and dogs and even insects immediately hit back if others try to harm them. A human being is not the exception.
Even if a law prohibits to use violence, one will surely hit back and defend himself, as otherwise he may lose his life. For a man to defend his body is not based on "the right" that is provided by the nation. In the case of a nation, for her to protect her existence is not because the Constitution provides its right to her or any international law authorize her to do so.

Is there any nation who bothers to write the right of her own defense in her own Constitution, though it is usual that the Constitution defines who declares the war, who is the head of the military forces, who has the authority to close the war, etc.

Let us assume that a Constitution denies any right of defense and stipulates as "forever renounce war as a sovereign right of the nation and the threat or use of force as means of settling international disputes as well as means to defend the country." plus "do not fight against the aggression from other nations"

Suppose that people of other country invade us actually, how do we act? The state would surely fight to protect her nationals. Possibly all nationals headed by policemen and coastal guard try to prevent the enemy.

That is a fairly tale and in reality, the Constitution does not deny for the nationals to protect the nation. Therefore Japan has the Self-Defense Force(originally, Police Reserve Force, later Peace Keeping Force) in order to stop the invasion from other nations.

Japanese Self-Defense Force(=JSDF) is established based on the JSDF Law enacted by the Diet and is not the forces to settle international disputes as defined by Constitution Art.9. It does not defy the stipulations of the Constitution as a matter of course.

We do not use force to settle international disputes. On the other hand, we prepare Self-Defense Forces in order to stop invasion from other countries. This present Japanese system with the record of continued peace for more than half century is Japan's proud in the world as the peaceful nation.

Putting the self-defense right in the clause of the Constitution, which is not necessary, cannot be the reason for the reform of the Constitution which has a proud history and results of more than 70 years.

The Constitution of Japan (excerpt)

Article 9.(RENUNCIATION OF WAR)

Aspiring sincerely to an international peace based on justice and order, the Japanese people forever renounce war as a sovereign right of the nation and the threat or use of force as means of settling international disputes.

In order to accomplish the aim of the preceding paragraph, land, sea, and air forces, as well as other war potential, will never be maintained. The right of belligerency of the state will not be recognized.

5. Constitution Art.9 is not almighty

Q5.

We cannot keep Japan's peace and security only by Constitution Art. 9. Actually, our northern territory and Takeshima Island are occupied by other countries and now Senkaku Islands are about to be invaded by China.   Should we not revise Art. 9 as soon as possible so as to acquire our own military forces like other countries ?

A5.

You cannot secure the peace of the nation just by keeping Article 9 of the Constitution. You can achieve nation's peace only through the strong will of the people on the basis of the clause of Article 9.

For the past 70 years when many people around the world have been involved in some kind of war, why the Japanese people could have escaped from any disaster?

It owes to the "Self-Defense Forces", one of the top-ten powers in the world, established by Self-Defense Force Law and the existence of the Japan-U.S. mutual security pact.   But more than anything else the people's strong will to be faithful to the principles of Japan's peaceful Constitution.

In other words, JSDF who are always engaged in the hard drilling with the firm will to defend the nation plus the backing of huge U.S. military forces who can join the operation with JSDF based upon the Japan-U.S. Security Treaty, have made it difficult for other nations to wage a war in Japan.   As a matter of fact, such an enemy did not appear over the past 70 more years.

In 1950-53 Korean War in spite of the strong pressure from our friendly allies United States Japan did not send JSDF(then Police Reserve Forces, after 1951 Peace Keeping Forces) in defiance of Constitution Art. 9.

Later on, our friendly allies United States have engaged in Vietnam War, various Middle-East Wars, Iraqi War, Anti-Terrorism War, Afghan Invasion, etc., but Japan has not been involved in them, keeping peace by unilateral Japan-US Security Treaty based on Constitution Art. 9.

In general wars between nations are wars of Justice vs. justice. In modern ages those are "national defense" vs. "national defense".

Over the past 65 years the U.S. has been fighting wars always outside her territory. For the antiestablishment people of the country which is attacked by the U.S. armed forces, the U.S. are the invader and the people are compelled to fight against the U.S. forces trying to oust them from their country by all means. But on the contrary the firm conviction of the U.S. is to protect world freedom and justice and do not hesitate to fight in other territory in order to secure the life and security of the citizens of that country. Of course, among U.S. allies there is no understanding of invading other countries at all.

United Kingdom, Canada, France, Spain, the Netherlands and other West European countries, China, Russia and almost all other nations except Japan acknowledge the authority (governors) to mobilize their armed forces when needed, and in international society each country does diplomatic negotiations upon that understanding. Accordingly, in reality the government may mobilize the troops urgently at the discretion of the authority.

So, it goes without saying that innumerable numbers of young people, non-combatant civilians have been killed in these battles. However, Japan has no such armed forces that the authority can mobilize. In other words, Japanese citizens have not been compelled to engage in any war by force of those in power under the stipulation of Constitution Art.9.

Thus, on one hand we never intervene the conflict between other countries under Constitution Art.9, we maintain, on the other, the strong police force (Police, Maritime Coastal Guard) and self-defense force(JSDF) against any invasion from other powers. With the tremendous continued efforts of those people concerned we have enjoyed the peace of Japan for long years.

Although we have a strong self-defense force, we must consider deliberately how to cope with such territorial problems as Northern Territories, Takeshima, Senkaku Islands, and decide the way to act properly in accordance with Art.9 which determines the peaceful settlement.

　It is hoped that people do not relate the difficult territorial problems with Constitution Art.9 and they should be more sensitive to the present current of society to change this article which is the world-leading clause to renounce not only the war but also the armed forces.

Self-Defense Forces Act

Act No. 165 of 1954

This law is not translated. The Japanese data is here.

(e-gov system)

自衛隊法　(抜粋)
（この法律の目的）
第一条　この法律は、自衛隊の任務、自衛隊の部隊の組織及び編成、自衛隊の行動及び権限、隊員の身分取扱等を定めることを目的とする。
（定義）
第二条　この法律において「自衛隊」とは、防衛大臣、防衛副大臣、防衛大臣政務官、防衛大臣補佐官、防衛大臣政策参与及び防衛大臣秘書官並びに防衛省の事務次官及び防衛審議官並びに防衛省本省の内部部局、防衛大学校、防衛医科大学校、防衛会議、統合幕僚監部、情報本部、防衛監察本部、地方防衛局その他の機関（政令で定める合議制の機関並びに防衛省設置法（昭和二十九年法律第百六十四号）第四条第一項第二十四号　又は第二十五号に掲げる事務をつかさどる部局及び職で政令で定めるものを除く。）並びに陸上自衛隊、海上自衛隊及び航空自衛隊並びに防衛装備庁（政令で定める合議制の機関を除く。）を含むものとする。
2　この法律において「陸上自衛隊」とは、陸上幕僚監部並びに統合幕僚長及び陸上幕僚長の監督を受ける部隊及び機関を含むものとする。
3　この法律において「海上自衛隊」とは、海上幕僚監部並びに統合幕僚長及び海上幕僚長の監督を受ける部隊及び機関を含むものとする。

4　この法律において「航空自衛隊」とは、航空幕僚監部並びに統合幕僚長及び航空幕僚長の監督を受ける部隊及び機関を含むものとする。
5　この法律(第九十四条の七第三号を除く。)において「隊員」とは、防衛省の職員で、防衛大臣、防衛副大臣、防衛大臣政務官、防衛大臣補佐官、防衛大臣政策参与、防衛大臣秘書官、第一項の政令で定める合議制の機関の委員、同項の政令で定める部局に勤務する職員及び同項の政令で定める職にある職員以外のものをいうものとする。
（自衛隊の任務）
第三条　自衛隊は、我が国の平和と独立を守り、国の安全を保つため、我が国を防衛することを主たる任務とし、必要に応じ、公共の秩序の維持に当たるものとする。
2　自衛隊は、前項に規定するもののほか、同項の主たる任務の遂行に支障を生じない限度において、かつ、武力による威嚇又は武力の行使に当たらない範囲において、次に掲げる活動であつて、別に法律で定めるところにより自衛隊が実施することとされるものを行うことを任務とする。
一　我が国の平和及び安全に重要な影響を与える事態に対応して行う我が国の平和及び安全の確保に資する活動
二　国際連合を中心とした国際平和のための取組への寄与その他の国際協力の推進を通じて我が国を含む国際社会の平和及び安全の維持に資する活動
3　陸上自衛隊は主として陸において、海上自衛隊は主として海において、航空自衛隊は主として空においてそれぞれ行動することを任務とする。

6. Article 9 is the results of earnest argument at the Imperial Diet

Q6.

The debate at the Imperial Parliament under occupation of the Allied Powers was a formal one. The clauses of the Constitution are merely compelled by the Supreme Commander for the Allied Powers. They should be amended immediately.

A6.

The Imperial Diet started the deliberation of the Constitution on June 21, 1946 based on the Constitutional amendment Guidance announced by the government of March 6, 1946. After the question and answer session in both general assembly and the special committee of the Imperial Diet, detailed discussion was held in the small committee to resolve the final draft.

Those members of the Diet are all chosen by the general election and no one was selected by the occupation forces. The draft of the constitution was exactly determined by the representatives of the Japanese nationals who kept various opinions reflecting the post-war society and is not the product of simple pressure of the occupation forces.

Reading the numerous pages of the minutes is a daunting task, but as an example the question and answer between Communist Party leader Nosaka Sanzo and Prime Minister Yoshida Shigeru draws interest.

At the 6/28/1946 Council, Nosaka Sanzo of Communist Party questioned:" There are two kinds of war in our opinion. One is an evil war such as the consecutive wars following the Manchurian Incident that Japan's imperialist committed. War conquering other nation ---, war of aggression ---; those are not justified. However, when a country is invaded, the war which the country opens against the aggressor is a just war. In the last War, China and/or US-Britain allied forces fought defensive war. We can say that was a just war. Is not it more accurate to write "the abandonment of invasion war" instead of "the abandonment of war" as expressed in the constitution draft? "

To it Yoshida Shigeru answered: "··· In the terms and conditions of the renouncing war, to justify the war as the use of national self-defense right is nothing but a harmful opinion. (applause) It is a clear fact that recent wars are fought in the name of national defense right. Therefore, to justify the self-defense right leads to let the war happen. Our next clause of belligerent rights waiver aims to establish an international peace organization. It aims to restrain all wars by establishing international peace organization. However, if ever there exists a self-defense war, we must assume the existence of a nation seeking invasion to other nations. Therefore, to admit the self-defense, i.e. the war using defense right easily lead to trigger the war itself. If and when a peace organization or such international organization is established, to acknowledge self-defense right is harmful in itself. Such opinions are hazardous and fruitless, I believe."

Yoshida refuted Nosaka's claim based on the historical facts that every war has been fought under the pretext of national defense. He stressed that once the peace organization (he thought something like the World Government) is established, National defense right becomes only harmful.   However, the similar questions as Nosaka raised were repeated by Hara Fujiro of the Progressive Party and various other Diet Members, all of which served to deepen the argument.

Then in the progress of deliberation Ashida Hitoshi, Chairman of the working group of the Special Committee for Constitutional Reform in the House of Representatives, presented an amendment to add to the original draft the clauses "Aspiring sincerely to an international peace based on justice and order," and "In order to accomplish the aim of the preceding paragraph."
With these amendments together with the sentences "the Japanese people forever renounce war as a sovereign right of the nation and the threat or use of force as means of settling international disputes" and "land, sea, and air forces, as well as other war potential, will never be maintained. The right of belligerency of the state will not be recognized", unprecedented Art.9 of the Constitution was achieved as in the present form.

Under this article Japanese people are in a position to request to the Power(rulers) that any international disputes should be settled not by means of war but by the peaceful means as diplomatic negotiations. Japanese people thus succeeded to apply brakes to government keeping armed forces for fighting wars.

On the other hands the World Government which Yoshida Shigeru aspired was not realized and the United Nations, which was created under the leadership of the victorious nations, always respect the sovereignty of member nations and not regulates them. So in reality fighting among sovereignty nations has been happening continuously. If other nations happen to invade Japan, we must fight against them otherwise we shall lose our existence or independence.

It is very clear that Japan cannot protect her broad islands only by her police forces. Hence, Japan started to maintain Self-Defense Forces, whose real power has been strengthened year after year in accordance with the reconstruction of the nation. But even when her fighting ability becomes high, as long as Article 9 exists, the Power (Ruler) cannot move over the intention of this article.

The Power(Ruler), whose power is limited by the constitution, have exerted their efforts to get out of this limit, so as to be able to order the JSDF more freely, aims to amend constitution. But from the viewpoint of the people in general, they wish to maintain the present situation as it is.

7. Strengthening JSDF is not a constitutional problem

Q7.

In view of the tense situation of Far East, we should Change the sentence of Art.9 to express the maintenance of Self-Defense Forces clearly so that the nationals understand easily the international situations.

A7.

It is a matter of course that Japan defend her country by herself. Not a few people argue that we should clearly put that sentence in the Constitution, which is more understandable to all nationals. We have to be very careful that there are some influential people who wish to change the principles of the Constitution like abolition of armed forces, adoption of imperial system, etc. taking this opportunity.

The Power(the Rulers) are tempted to change Article 9 so as to have the armed forces as other nations have for settling international disputes by force (whether it is "self-defense forces" or "national defense force" is not a question so far as it is an armed forces that can be mobilized by the rulers).

For example, at the United Nations when other countries are united to solve the international disputes by using forces "to defend justice", Japan cannot participate in the movement ・・・ we can imagine how sorry our diplomats feel at such instances.

Especially when they cannot respond to the strong request from our most friendly nation such as the United States, they fear a possible disturbance to the cooperative spirit of the two nations.

If Japan had had the armed forces similar to other countries' since 1960s, we could have sent or troops to Vietnam, Middle East, Iraq, Syria, Afghanistan, Africa, etc. as a fulfilment of "international cooperation" (and at the same time many Japanese people must have experienced an endless agony as the results of participation of those wars.)

Also at against the North Korean abduction cases, the border problems like Senkaku, Takeshima, Northern Territories, etc, the government could have acted more strongly to the relative nations and could have escaped from being criticized by the public so widely.

On the top of those, if, being urged by the constitutional reform, the government get out of Japan's three principles controlling arms exports, the Japanese war industry can revive its old vigor.

On the other hand, the anti-Japanese feeling would grow more highly in China, Russia and Korea and the Japanese military power would be enlarged accordingly.

The United States, who are being worried about everlasting expansion of her military budget, will surely welcome those Japanese policy changes, and the reshuffling of Japan-US Alliance(realization of mutual military alliance) and the US Far East Armed Forces are to be gradually replaced by the Japanese Forces.

There are many countries in the world where the Constitution stipulates who declares the war (the national assembly, the president, the king, the emperor, the Chief Justice, the prime minister, or else), or who ends the war, or who command the armed forces.
However there is no nation in the world where the constitution determine such a simple theory like "the nationals defend the country", or "the nation has the defense right", or "nationals have duty to defend the country", etc. isn't there?

I think the fact that such opinion of putting the defense duty in the constitution is so prevailing in Japan today shows the people's dependent nature on the central government.
The world would take all Japanese people are like that if such stipulation appears in the revised version of Japanese Constitution.

Of course, in reality, our national Diet determined JSDF Law under the present constitution and for more than a half century we have kept Self-Defense Forces, who have served to protect our country spending one of world's 10 largest annual defense budgets, which has made our country most peaceful nation in the world. As a matter of fact, backed by the Japan-US Security Treaty, even Chinese Peoples' Liberation Army seem unable to invade Senkaku islands using their belligerent right.

If we are to cope with the uneasy situations of Far East, important is not the constitutional reform but the adjustment of the relative defense regulations and the strengthening of defense power of JSDF.

8. JSDF is not an armed forces

Q8.
 JSDF is an armed force from every point of view.　No one in the world believe it is not armed forces.　JSDF is apparently inconsistent with Article 9 of the Japanese Constitution. We must amend the Article 9 to put JSDF back to normal to suit the stipulation of the constitution.

A8.
 Through the bitter experience of the Great East Asian War, we Japanese determined to renounce war eternally as means of settling international disputes, and on the top of it we decided to　never maintain armed forces first time in world history.

 JSDF as established under the stipulation of the Constitution is determined by Article 3 of JSDF Law passed at the Diet is destined to protect the country from the evasion of other nations and definitely is not an armed force that the Article 9 of the Constitution decided not to maintain as means to settle the international disputes.

 In the case of other nation's armed forces, they are the forces that the Power (the Rulers) can at any time when he judges it necessary to protect the country may order to fight regardless of the naming of the forces like the National Guard, National Defense Fores, Peoples' Liberation Army, etc.

 As a matter of fact, since the end of WWII, those armed forces have been continuously mobilized by their government to fight and kill others in the name of protect national interest or to oppress the anti-government forces.

 Meantime, the peaceful constitution that Japan established after the War clearly put obstacle to the Power (the Rulers) with easy expression and as the results for over a half century our country has never participated in any war and the government has never used armed forces to suppress any anti-government movement.

Those people who do not have the similar constitution like Japanese are continuing to have the conventional armed forces apt to think that JSDF are the same establishment as their own armed forces. It may be natural for them to think in such a way as they have never experienced such constitution as Japanese have. Even many of the Japanese people themselves do not understand the true meaning of Article 9. Also, some Japanese politicians wish to change this article to become able to have armed forces similar to those of other nations.

Actually there are more countries where the National Defense Army fight against their own citizens rather than fighting against other nationals. If ever those countries maintain the similar constitutions like the Japanese Constitution and do not maintain armed forces, it will help to serve the stoppage of the present killing occurring everywhere in the world.

We should be more proud and confident with our post-war history and our constitution and explain to the world that in Japan no armed forces exist and JSDF solely aim to protect the country against the invasion of other country. To plea the fundamental thinking of the peaceful constitution to the people of the world is the best contribution to the international society for the achievement of world peace.

Chapter 3 Emperor: Symbol of Japan

9. The Emperor is not the sovereign of Japan

Q9,
The Emperor is determined to be the symbol of Japan in accordance with the present Constitution. The word "symbol" is not a genuine Japanese word but is a translation from English. The Emperor should be the sovereign of Japan like other countries.

A9.
  To call a person who perform only such acts in matters of state as are specified in Art. 7 of the Constitution "the sovereign" sounds somewhat strange.
  If it is convenient to call the Emperor the sovereign as LDP says, keeping his function as it is today, then the Diet （Supreme national organization） may set up a law to determine the Emperor as the sovereign or the Head of the State. Then the foreign people other than the experts do not notice that the Japanese sovereign performs only such acts as specified in Art.7.

This may be convenient as LDP politicians say, but soon people of the foreign countries begin to doubt if such a person is the sovereign or not.

  Then the domestic monarchists would start arguing that the Emperor should have the authority similar to that of the other countries' sovereigns.

  It is easily estimated that such thought as "The Emperor is sacred and inviolable." ,"The sovereign of Japan is the Emperor", or "The Emperor declares war", etc. etc. would gradually prevail.

  That the article 1 of the present Constitution stipulates "The Emperor shall be the symbol of the State and of the unity of the People," means that the Japanese people understand such abstract notion as the state and/or the unity of the people through "the Emperor." It is very clear that the Emperor is not the sovereign who expresses the national will.

In the Imperial Constitution, the Emperor is the sovereign who reign over the Empire of Japan, but in the Constitution of Japan the sovereign power resides with the people of Japan. And the Emperor's position as the symbol of Japan and of the unity of the people derives from the will of the Japanese people and not combines in Himself the rights of sovereignty.

In the Imperial Constitution, the position of the Emperor is proper to the Emperor by a line of Emperors unbroken for ages eternal. It was also stipulated that the Emperor is the sovereign of the state who exercises the legislative, the administrative and the jurisdiction powers. Whether he is "the symbol" or "the sovereign" is not simply the question of the word.

The Imperial Constitution of Japan 1889
(Excerpts)

ARTICLE I. The Empire of Japan shall be reigned over and governed by a line of Emperors unbroken for ages eternal.

ARTICLE III. The Emperor is sacred and inviolable.
ARTICLE IV. The Emperor is the head of the Empire, combining in Himself the rights of sovereignty, and exercises them, according to the provisions of the present Constitution.
ARTICLE V. The Emperor exercises the legislative power with the consent of the Imperial Diet.
ARTICLE VI. The Emperor gives sanction to laws and orders them to be promulgated and executed.

ARTICLE XI. The Emperor has the supreme command of the Army and Navy.

ARTICLE XIII. The Emperor declares war, makes peace, and concludes treaties.

ARTICLE LVII. The Judicature shall be exercised by the Courts of Law according to law, in the name of the Emperor.

The organization of the Courts of Law shall be determined by law.

The Constitution of Japan 1947
(Excerpts)

Article 1. The Emperor shall be the symbol of the State and of the unity of the People, deriving his position from the will of the people with whom resides sovereign power.

Article 4. The Emperor shall perform only such acts in matters of state as are provided for in this Constitution and he shall not have powers related to government.
The Emperor may delegate the performance of his acts in matters of state as may be provided by law.

LDP's Draft of the Revised Constitution of Japan 2012
(Excerpts)

Article 1. The Emperor shall be the sovereign and the symbol of the State and of the unity of the People, deriving his position from the will of the people with whom resides sovereign power.

Article 5. The Emperor shall perform only such acts in matters of state as are provided for in this Constitution and he shall not have powers related to government.

Chapter 4 Necessity to change Article 9

10. Constitutional stipulation is inconvenient to the government

Q10.
What are the inconvenience to the people if Article 9 is not changed?

A10.
As there are only few nations that have the constitution of renunciation of war and strictly defensive national security policy, those who feel the inconvenience from Article 9 are mainly the Japanese diplomats working in the United Nations and the other international conferences.

The English translation for JSDF established under the regulation of Article 9 is "Self Defense Forces", but they are often translated to Japanese Military forces or simply Japanese Army.　The reason for that is that many of those who use English language do not understand Article 9 (even in Japan not a few politicians, bureaucrats, scholars, commentators believe that JSDF are the armed forces)

Therefore, when in the United Nations the countries agree to send their armies to somewhere in the world, only Japan cannot join the common front, which make the other countries question why such a country keeping world 10 big army do not send her army.　They often criticize Japan as a country who only sends money but no blood.

But on the other hand, the existence of Japanese Self-Defense Forces, i.e. JGSDF(Japanese Ground Self-Defense Force http://www.mod.go.jp/gsdf/)、JMSDF(Japanese Maritime Self-Defense Force http://www.mod.go.jp/msdf/)、JASDF(Japanese Air Self-Defense Force http://www.mod.go.jp/asdf/)　are nowadays widely understood in the world as the organizations established for strictly defensive purpose unlike the conventional armed forces.　In domestic criminal law "self-defense" is completely lawful action that one can act.

It is quite natural that some Japanese diplomats tend to hope for the abolition of article 9 so as to go along equally with other countries in international politics, though they should take hard time in explaining the Japanese people's intention embodied in Article 9.　The politicians also, when they are criticized by the people in general for their timid attitude to their counterparts in case of North-Korean diplomatic relations, the territorial issues, economic problems with foreign countries, feel vexed for having the stipulations of Article 9.

From this viewpoint, it is quite understandable that the recent constitutional reform argument is presented mainly from the Power (the rulers) not from the people in general.

And the continuous actions of the Power(the rulers) with their loud voices is now causing the mind of the people towards constitutional reform. The LDP draft for the new constitution has been worked out in the course of this current.

11. Let us be proud of and have confidence in our constitution

Q11.
In the face of various international disputes frequently happening everywhere in the world, nations in the world are cooperating to send their own troops to settle the problems. Japan will become excluded from the world family if she continues to be ignorant of the happenings with the shield of her constitution. Should we not do our own duty of international cooperation by revising Article 9 of our Constitution?

A11.
 After WWⅡ, we abandoned the armed forces as a means of settling international disputes, and in addition created a world-leading army renunciation clause on Article 9 of the Constitution. Invasion-war-waiver provisions are employed by many countries in the world, but those seldom go further to the total renunciation of the armed forces.

 Next year is 70 years after the War. Due to this thorough constitutional provisions, until now, JSDF(Japanese Self-Defense Forces) have never participated in any wars between other countries and also never used forces to the public in anti-Government demonstrations and activities. Although JSDF keep appropriate powers in preparations for the threat of neighboring military nations, they are fundamentally different from armed forces of other countries.

 The Shinzo Abe administration decided as the cabinet decision that the government can mobilize JSDF into the war between other countries by way of using the collective self-defense right in line with the armed forces of other countries. We wish to judge this political movement with the fair understanding of the realities of international politics, and to keep being proud of and confident in our post-war history and the constitution that we have established.

(from Tokyo Shimbun "HATUGEN(Remark)" 2014 / 8 / 1 Kato Yasuya, 77 - year-old, Retired)

In real wars where the hostile nations collide with each other using their full power, it is quite natural that one regards the third party who stand with another party to support as a hostile nation. One would surely fight this third party to stop the aid activities.

JSDF, which is engaged in the aid activities in Japan's own judgment on the site where they are actually fighting, may possibly be attacked by a warring party. Especially, when JSDF are in fueling or mine removal activities, such danger will become more increased. JSDF are forced to fight to protect themselves if and when they are attacked, and as the results Japan become involved in the war as a matter of course.

For a neutral country to be not involved in the war she should not approach the combat zone, which is the fundamental principles of international politics and international law. How many Japanese people wish to throw away the constitution clause that they themselves have kept to secure peace and to adopt the new clause of other countries who still keep conventional armed forces and who are always in danger of getting involved in wars of other countries?

11. Cabinet decision does not change the Constitutional clause

Q11.
The Abe Cabinet's decision of July 1, 2014 to change the interpretation of the Constitution clearly specifies as follows:
 (A) We do not perform aid activities where the armed forces of the aid-target nation are "actually engaged in war activities."
 (B) If the situations change and the site where we are performing the aid activities becomes the site where the armed forces of the aid-target nation are "actually engaged in war activities", we immediately stop or suspend the aid activities there.

　Therefore, there is no fear for JSDF would become involved in any war as long as the Article 9 of the Constitution is not reformed.　　Isn't it correct?

A11.
　The conditions expressed in the Cabinet Decision does not apply the brakes for the country to get involved in the war.
　Because if the armed forces of the warring party attack as hostile forces JSDF who are engaged in the aid activities at the "site where they are not actually performing battle", JSDF must fight against the attack in order to protect their safety, although they immediately stop or suspend their aid activities according to the Cabinet Decision.

　Accordingly, although in the Japanese view the nation is working "aid activities", if in the eyes of the other side the activities are interpreted as hostile, the battle starts between Japan and the other party.　　The site immediately changes into the "site where the battles are actually occurring."

　Thus even when the constitution so clearly stipulates the clause using the examples, it is impossible to say that the government(the Powers) do not override what the constitution stipulates.

The dispatch of JSDF squad to Samawah, Iraq was carried out by Junichiro Koizumi Cabinet for the reason that the site was not a battlefield but so dangerous that no Japanese other than JSDF could be engaged in the repair works there. They are not sent in order to engage in the war activities.

But legally their action very possibly defy with the Art. 3 Sect.1 of JSDF Law which says "The aim of JSDF is to protect nation's peace and independence and to keep nation's safety defending our country as well as , if necessary, engage in the work of keeping the public order."

If a member of JSDF filed a suit for compensatory damages against the government, the results would have been very hard to imagine.   However, for the time being the government action has widely been accepted by the people in general and in July, 2014 the interpretation change of article 9 of the constitution by the Cabinet Decision and the reform of the relative laws that followed is supposed to be in the same context.

Now, what the Powers (the government) wish to go one more step to participate in the war which Japan's ally is fighting as an execution of the "collective defense right" on the supposition that there are two types of defense right, i.e. "the individual defense right" and "the collective defense right". The government position is to dispatch JSDF to the war in which the US is one party on the understanding that such action is constitutional.

On July 1, 2014, Shinzo Abe Cabinet decided the new interpretation of the constitution that it does not prohibit the dispatch of JSDF to such a site where the war is not fought actually.   The Diet then after revised the relative laws accordingly.

But, whether this decision was just or not legally is very difficult to preview before the Jurisdiction will present her view officially.   Or, maybe the majority of Japanese people in general support Abe Cabinet view.   Then the articles of the constitution will be changed by the plebiscite before the matter would go to the Supreme Court.

12. What is the aim of LDP draft of constitutional reform ?

Q12.
The LDP draft of constitutional reform clearly stipulates the self-defense right and the foundation of National Defense Forces, which are necessary for the present age. What is the problem for such a plan to clarify the ambiguous expression of the constitution now in force ?

A12.
The LDP draft of constitutional reform stipulates in Art.9 to maintain "defense right "and in 2nd section of Art. 9 obligates the Power (the government) to establish "the National Defense Forces"

When this draft is realized, the government becomes free from the principles that any international dispute must be settled peacefully. Thus the government can threat or use the national defense forces in order to settle such international disputes at their judgement, and the government will have more variety of choices in international politics.

Even if the Japanese homeland is not attacked, the long-fetched idea of LDP i.e. <the nation is given the right to use the defense right by the people → for Japan to fight a war against the enemy of Japan's ally (USA) is recognized by the constitution as the use of "collective defense right" → moreover in Sect.2 of Art.9 "National Defense Force" is admitted as a constitutional establishment, of which the supreme commander is the Prime Minister → the Prime Minister is in a position to dispatch the Defense Force to overseas (e.g. the Middle East) at the request of the ally (e.g. USA)> now becomes realized.

At this moment, many politicians claim that the constitutional reform only gives a freehand to the government, so that even when USA request the dispatch the Defense Forces to where USA want, Japanese Government can deny the request and this does not mean the immediate dispatch of the Defense Forces abroad. They say, "Just believe us !!"

However we can hardly believe that many Japanese people who experienced the severe results of giving freehand to the Power (the government), which finally led them to the Great East Asian War.　Actually, from that experience the article 9 of the Constitution was created.

In September, 2014, for the war against ISIS who aimed to unify Syria and Iraq, divided in to two by Anglo-French secret agreement, the United States advocated the establishment of the Coalition Ally together with main nations of the NATO, i.e. UK, France, Germany, Italy, Canada, Australia, Turkey, Poland and Denmark.

Then after ISIS in cooperation with anti-Asad power enlarged their sphere in Syria remarkably.　Now Russia is supporting Asad regime in the aim to destroy ISIS, while US, who plan to eliminate Asad regime, support anti-Asad power and try to destroy ISIS. At this point Japan with the realization of the new security system has the way to be able to be engaged in the military cooperation with US if US requests her to do so.

LDP Draft of the Constitutional Reform (April 27, 2012)
https://jimin.ncss.nifty.com/pdf/news/policy/130250_1.pdf

Chapter 5   National Defense and the Japan-US Security Treaty

13. The Japan-US Security Treaty, the results of the benefits of both nations

Q13.

Japan-US Security Treaty is a unilateral contract which stipulates the US duty to protect Japan but does not specify Japanese duty to protect US.   Japan must change Article 9 of the Constitution so as to establish the armed forces as other nations have, and change the Japan-US Security Treaty to be bilateral, thus to become a true independent nation.

A13

The Article 9 of the Constitution deliberately specifies the renunciation of war as means of settling international disputes with the very clear expression of "land, sea, and air forces, as well as other war potential, will never be maintained." However, the article does not deny the self-defense of the nation at all.   As was made clear in A4, such phrase is of character that is not to be defined in any law.

Japan established the Self-Defense Forces Law under this constitution and put to JSDF "the main duty of defend the country" in order to "maintain the peace and independence of the country and keep nation's safety"

The present problem is the current of the times that the people just leave everything about the national defense to JSDF, and it is always an important issue to deepen and elevate the understanding and awareness of the duty and importance of JSDF.   For the politicians failing to exert such efforts just to shout the constitutional reform is like barking up the wrong tree.

The Japan-US Security Treaty is a treaty as agreed completely for the interests of the both nations.   The United States acquire the right of stationing

their troops on the land of Japan in exchange for the duty to protect the nation together with the Japanese people.
Japan took the benefit of the US Armed Forces to cover the insufficient capacity of JSDF, and the US took the benefit of continuing the stationing of her Armed Forces on the land of Japan in the course of her worldwide strategy. That is the perfect Win-Win bilateral treaty.

However some people claim that to let the US unilaterally protect Japan by "Japan-US Security Treaty"for the national security is such a selfish thinking as not to be justified for long. They even incite people to cancel the treaty in order for Japan to acquire true independence.

Do they think that the post-war US is just engaged in the defense of Japan without any compensation? Isn't it more correct that the US decided to sign the treaty because they secured their interest? Isn't it correct that Japan, on the other side, let the US take part of the Japanese defense in exchange of admitting the stationing of US troop in Japan as the results of the clever diplomacy led by Shigeru Yoshida, a long-experienced diplomat and politician.

Following the opinions of those people, if we cancel the "Japan-US Security Treaty", establish "our own constitution" which allows the maintenance of the same armed forces as other countries and change JSDF to "National Defense Forces", it is very doubtful whether we can keep or peace and safety as we enjoyed for the past half century.

There are many important points cleverly inserted in the LDP draft of constitutional reform. If the power (the government) really think the national defense, there are an amount of actions they should take immediately. They shelve or suspend all those troublesome actions and just shout " JSDF is unconstitutional !! ", "Reform the constitution !!", which are very easy to the ears of the people in general.

Take for example the territorial issues. It is very much necessary to appeal to international sentiment by filing suit to international court of justice. Such a steady and slow step and preparation has not been advanced.   As for Senkaku problem, the government had left the island as a private land until Tokyo Governor Shintaro Ishihara raised the problem, and failed to continue the history of national occupation for long years.   Also, the complimentary regulations to the JSDF Law like the law relating to the activities of JSDF when the country is invaded, the cooperation system of the people (including the restriction of private right) at that time, detailed regulations of movement of heavy artillery, tanks, warplanes, warships, etc., all of which has been often remarked by the learned experts.   The powers (the government) just claim article 9 is the obstacle to do so.

The present constitution does not deny JSDF and such legislation to deal with emergencies is urgently needed for the national security.   Legislation is within the power of the Diet and does never defy with the constitution.

The constitution should determine the renunciation of the armed forces as the Japan under Meiji Constitution used to have or the most other nations of the world keep, and also determine Japan never uses forces to settle international disputes……… that is, article 9 of the present constitution.

We should be prouder of our post-war history and the constitution that we ourselves established.

TREATY OF MUTUAL COOPERATION AND SECURITY BETWEEN JAPAN AND THE UNITED STATES OF AMERICA (Extract)

ARTICLE III

The Parties, individually and in cooperation with each other, by means of continuous and effective self-help and mutual aid will maintain and develop, subject to their constitutional provisions, their capacities to resist armed attack.

ARTICLE IV

The Parties will consult together from time to time regarding the implementation of this Treaty, and, at the request of either Party, whenever the security of Japan or international peace and security in the Far East is threatened.

ARTICLE V

Each Party recognizes that an armed attack against either Party in the territories under the administration of Japan would be dangerous to its own peace and safety and declares that it would act to meet the common danger in accordance with its constitutional provisions and processes. Any such armed attack and all measures taken as a result thereof shall be immediately reported to the Security Council of the United Nations in accordance with the provisions of Article 51 of the Charter. Such measures shall be terminated when the Security Council has taken the measures necessary to restore and maintain international peace and security.

ARTICLE VI

For the purpose of contributing to the security of Japan and the maintenance of international peace and security in the Far East, the United States of America is granted the use by its land, air and naval forces of facilities and areas in Japan. The use of these facilities and areas as well as the status of United States armed forces in Japan shall be governed by a separate agreement, replacing the Administrative Agreement under Article III of the Security Treaty between Japan and the United States of America, signed at Tokyo on February 28, 1952, as amended, and by such other arrangements as may be agreed upon.

14. The collective defense right is the justification for the action taken in accordance with a military alliance

Q14.

 The security environment in the Far-east surrounding Japan is becoming increasingly severe due to the Chinese remarkable enhance of presence in the international community. It is impossible for Japan to protect the country only by herself. We should promptly change our constitution so as to admit the collective defense right and be ready to meet against Chinese aggression strengthening Japan-US alliance.

A14.

 The Liberal Democratic Party (LDP), whose final aim is to reform the constitution, with her cabinet decision of July 1, 2014 , played a leading role to revise the relative laws in order to enable the dispatch of JSDF to the war-field where the US is engaged in battles, on the interpretation that there are two kinds of "defense right", i.e. "individual defense right" and "collective defense right", and that to join the battle in which an allied nation is fighting does not defy the constitutional clause because such action is an effect of "collective defense force".

 However, when the Cabinet's interpretation of constitution is referred to the judgement of the jurisdiction, it is quite clear that the action is a violation of Article 9 of the Constitution.   It is anticipated that LDP cabinet will strengthen her intervention on the Supreme Court and also on the mass media.

 The present LDP draft of constitutional reform stipulates clearly the maintenance of "defense right", which is not mentioned in Article 9 of the present constitution, and it makes it a duty for the government to establish the "National Defense Forces" in Section 2.   Once this draft is enacted, the power(the government) is no more restricted to send JSDF legally to the battlefield of other nations.

<The nation is granted "defense right" by the people in accordance with the constitution→To join the war against the enemy of Japan's ally (USA) is authorized by the constitution as "collective defense right"→in its Section 2 "National Defense Forces" with the Prime Minister as the supreme commander is legalized by the Constitution → On the request of the ally (USA), the Prime Minister orders the dispatch of National Defense Forces to the battlefield (e.g. Afghanistan, Middle-East, etc.)> ···· this long-cherished idea of the power (the government) will now be realized.

Many politicians of ruling party as well as opposition party argue that under such reformed constitution the power (the government) just keep the free-hand and not necessarily follow the request from US but is in a position to reject it, therefore the constitutional reform does not directly mean the dispatch of the defense forces to overseas. They say that people should believe the politicians more strongly. However many Japanese people cannot easily believe those politicians as they experienced how dangerous it is to let the free-hand to the power(the government) at the last Great East-Asian War. Actually, for that very reason the Article 9 of the constitution was created.

Chapter 6 About the Collective Defense Right

15. The Article 9 of the Constitution does not admit the attack to other nation on the grounds of alliance treaty

Q15.

In "Defense Right", there are "individual defense right" and "collective defense right", and every nation in the world enjoy both rights, which is recognized by the United Nations Charter. Isn't it strange to say that only Japan can exercise "individual defense right" and not "collective defense right" ?

A15

(1) According to Article 39 to 50 of the Charter of United Nations, the Security Council determines the existence of breach of the peace or act of aggression and request the parties concerned to comply with the provisional measures that the Security Council decides. Meanwhile the Security Council may request the members of UN to take various measures like the interruption of economic relations, etc. not involving the use of armed forces. And if such measures prove to be inadequate, the Security Council may take military actions using the armed forces of UN member nations.

But until the UN takes such necessary measures the attacked nation must defend her homeland by herself.

Therefore Article 51 of the Charter admits exercising her right of individual or collective self-defense until the Security Council has taken the necessary measures.

(2) In case Japan is invaded by other nations, she immediately refers the problem to the Security Council.

However, if the attacking nation is a permanent member of the Security Council as China or Russia, who surely denies her invasion and exercises veto to the Japanese plea, no decision is expected in accordance with Article 39-50 and Japan must defend the country by her own forces.

If the attacking nation is a non-permanent member of the Security Council like the Republic of Korea , with the unanimous support of the permanent member of the Security Council there is a possibility that Articles 39-50 may be realized, but more possibility is that some of the permanent members of the Security Council exercise the veto to defend the position of the attacking nation. And as the results no decision is to be made in accordance to Article 39-50, thus Japan must defend the country by her own power using the defense right as the Article 51 defines.

In accordance with JSDF Law the JSDF will be engaged in the defense of the homeland.

At the same time, Japan request for the cooperation of US troop in accordance with the Japan-US Security Treaty as the use of collective defense right. And if the US accept that request, the both nations fight against the invaders together.

In accordance with Article 51 of the Charter, Japan's exercise of the right of self-defense shall be immediately reported to the Security Council, who does not deny the Japanese action.

(3) Now in case the US is invaded by other nation, the process is the same as (2), i.e. the US shall act using her defense right. But as unlike Japan the US keeps various military alliance with many other nations those allied countries shall come to participate in the war using their collective defense right.

As to the relations with Japan, Japan has no duty to join the war according to the Article 4 of Japan-US Security Treaty. From the first Japan does not have the military forces to settle the international disputes in accordance with Article 9 of her Constitution and the US is aware of this fact.   Nevertheless, based on the new constitutional interpretation on July 1, 2015 if Japan changes the laws relating JSDF and revises the Japan-US Security Treaty to the bilateral alliance

Treaty, it becomes possible that Japan can open war against the nation who invaded the US.

(4) The unilateral alliance relationship between Japan and the US that "when Japan is invaded, the US will help fighting against the invader, but when the US is invaded Japan does not help fighting against the invader" is the treaty agreed between two countries' national interest i.e. between Japan that wished to strengthen her safety without having armed forces, and the United States that wished to continue using her military bases in Japan in accordance with her world strategy. Therefore, the clauses of the Treaty were carefully made up based on the respect of the sovereignty of both nations not against the constitutions of both countries.

(5) The UN Charter also respect the sovereignty of the member nations in accordance with international law and does not deny each country's constitution as well as the alliance agreement agreed between the member nations. The United Nations is not the world government but the combination of the sovereign countries, so the UN Charter (which is the treaty international law binding the member nations) respect the sovereignty of member nations ad does not deny any alliance treaties agreed between each member nations.

If you understand this difference of internal law and international law, you will easily comprehend the past government's interpretation of the constitution based on the explanation of the Cabinet Legislation Bureau that " Japan does not have the Armed Forces to settle international disputes and renounced the right of belligerency in accordance with Article 9 of the Constitution, and so it is against the constitution for JSDF whose aim is the self−defense, to participate in the war of other nations who do not invade Japan".

Any clause of UN Charter which admit the self-defense right before the UN takes the collective defense action cannot be the reason to revise the world's most advanced Article 9 of the constitution.

CHARTER OF THE UNITED NATIONS (EXTRACT)

CHAPTER VI: PACIFIC SETTLEMENT OF DISPUTES

Article 33

1. The parties to any dispute, the continuance of which is likely to endanger the maintenance of international peace and security, shall, first of all, seek a solution by negotiation, enquiry, mediation, conciliation, arbitration, judicial settlement, resort to regional agencies or arrangements, or other peaceful means of their own choice.
2. The Security Council shall, when it deems necessary, call upon the parties to settle their dispute by such means.

Article 34

The Security Council may investigate any dispute, or any situation which might lead to international friction or give rise to a dispute, in order to determine whether the continuance of the dispute or situation is likely to endanger the maintenance of international peace and security.

Article 35

1. Any Member of the United Nations may bring any dispute, or any situation of the nature referred to in Article 34, to the attention of the Security Council or of the General Assembly.
2. A state which is not a Member of the United Nations may bring to the attention of the Security Council or of the General Assembly any dispute to which it is a party if it accepts in advance, for the purposes of the dispute, the obligations of pacific settlement provided in the present Charter.
3. The proceedings of the General Assembly in respect of matters brought to its attention under this Article will be subject to the provisions of Articles 11 and 12.

Article 36

1. The Security Council may, at any stage of a dispute of the nature referred to in Article 33 or of a situation of like nature, recommend appropriate procedures or methods of adjustment.
2. The Security Council should take into consideration any procedures for the settlement of the dispute which have already been adopted by the parties.

3. In making recommendations under this Article the Security Council should also take into consideration that legal disputes should as a general rule be referred by the parties to the International Court of Justice in accordance with the provisions of the Statute of the Court.

Article 37

1. Should the parties to a dispute of the nature referred to in Article 33 fail to settle it by the means indicated in that Article, they shall refer it to the Security Council.
2. If the Security Council deems that the continuance of the dispute is in fact likely to endanger the maintenance of international peace and security, it shall decide whether to take action under Article 36 or to recommend such terms of settlement as it may consider appropriate.

Article 38

Without prejudice to the provisions of Articles 33 to 37, the Security Council may, if all the parties to any dispute so request, make recommendations to the parties with a view to a pacific settlement of the dispute.

CHAPTER VII: ACTION WITH RESPECT TO THREATS TO THE PEACE, BREACHES OF THE PEACE, AND ACTS OF AGGRESSION

Article 39

The Security Council shall determine the existence of any threat to the peace, breach of the peace, or act of aggression and shall make recommendations, or decide what measures shall be taken in accordance with Articles 41 and 42, to maintain or restore international peace and security.

Article 40

In order to prevent an aggravation of the situation, the Security Council may, before making the recommendations or deciding upon the measures provided for in Article 39, call upon the parties concerned to comply with such provisional measures as it deems necessary or desirable. Such provisional measures shall be without prejudice to the rights, claims, or position of the parties concerned. The Security Council shall duly take account of failure to comply with such provisional measures.

Article 41

The Security Council may decide what measures not involving the use of armed force are to be employed to give effect to its decisions, and it may call upon the Members of the United Nations to apply such measures. These may include complete or partial interruption of economic relations and of rail, sea, air, postal, telegraphic, radio, and other means of communication, and the severance of diplomatic relations.

Article 42

Should the Security Council consider that measures provided for in Article 41 would be inadequate or have proved to be inadequate, it may take such action by air, sea, or land forces as may be necessary to maintain or restore international peace and security. Such action may include demonstrations, blockade, and other operations by air, sea, or land forces of Members of the United Nations.

Article 43

1. All Members of the United Nations, in order to contribute to the maintenance of international peace and security, undertake to make available to the Security Council, on its call and in accordance with a special agreement or agreements, armed forces, assistance, and facilities, including rights of passage, necessary for the purpose of maintaining international peace and security.
2. Such agreement or agreements shall govern the numbers and types of forces, their degree of readiness and general location, and the nature of the facilities and assistance to be provided.
3. The agreement or agreements shall be negotiated as soon as possible on the initiative of the Security Council. They shall be concluded between the Security Council and Members or between the Security Council and groups of Members and shall be subject to ratification by the signatory states in accordance with their respective constitutional processes.

Article 44

When the Security Council has decided to use force it shall, before calling upon a Member not represented on it to provide armed forces in fulfilment of the obligations assumed under Article 43, invite that Member, if the Member so desires, to participate in the decisions of the Security Council concerning the employment of contingents of that Member's armed forces.

Article 45

In order to enable the United Nations to take urgent military measures, Members shall hold immediately available national air-force contingents for combined international enforcement action. The strength and degree of readiness of these contingents and plans for their combined action shall be determined within the limits laid down in the special agreement or agreements referred to in Article 43, by the Security Council with the assistance of the Military Staff Committee.

Article 46

Plans for the application of armed force shall be made by the Security Council with the assistance of the Military Staff Committee.

Article 47

1. There shall be established a Military Staff Committee to advise and assist the Security Council on all questions relating to the Security Council's military requirements for the maintenance of international peace and security, the employment and command of forces placed at its disposal, the regulation of armaments, and possible disarmament.
2. The Military Staff Committee shall consist of the Chiefs of Staff of the permanent members of the Security Council or their representatives. Any Member of the United Nations not permanently represented on the Committee shall be invited by the Committee to be associated with it when the efficient discharge of the Committee's responsibilities requires the participation of that Member in its work.
3. The Military Staff Committee shall be responsible under the Security Council for the strategic direction of any armed forces placed at the disposal of the Security Council. Questions relating to the command of such forces shall be worked out subsequently.
4. The Military Staff Committee, with the authorization of the Security Council and after consultation with appropriate regional agencies, may establish regional sub-committees.

Article 48

1. The action required to carry out the decisions of the Security Council for the maintenance of international peace and security shall be taken by all the Members of the United Nations or by some of them, as the Security Council may determine.
2. Such decisions shall be carried out by the Members of the United Nations directly and through their action in the appropriate international agencies of which they are members.

Article 49

The Members of the United Nations shall join in affording mutual assistance in carrying out the measures decided upon by the Security Council.

Article 50

If preventive or enforcement measures against any state are taken by the Security Council, any other state, whether a Member of the United Nations or not, which finds itself confronted with special economic problems arising from the carrying out of those measures shall have the right to consult the Security Council with regard to a solution of those problems.

Article 51

Nothing in the present Charter shall impair the inherent right of individual or collective self-defence if an armed attack occurs against a Member of the United Nations, until the Security Council has taken measures necessary to maintain international peace and security. Measures taken by Members in the exercise of this right of self-defence shall be immediately reported to the Security Council and shall not in any way affect the authority and responsibility of the Security Council under the present Charter to take at any time such action as it deems necessary in order to maintain or restore international peace and security.

16. No nation invades the other

Q16.

The Japanese people who are used to peaceful circumstances should be more aware of the military threat of China and Russia.　They are always seeking chance to catch Japan off guard.　Shall Japan be in a dangerous situation if she continues to take the present position?

A16.

> (1) In international politics, an invading nation never admits that she is invading other nation.

She usually claims that her action is unavoidable to keep her safety against the invasion or to keep international peace and justice and that all the responsibility for the conflict should be borne by the nation invaded.　It is for this reason that the war is said to be a conflict between "justice" and "justice".

In UN Charter, if the Security Council recognizes the act of aggression, the object nation is determined as an aggressor, but without such decision of the Security Council both countries related to the dispute continue to claim that the other nation is an aggressor, and the allied nations of the both sides come to join the war as an action to execute collective defense right.　Then the war spreads more and more.

History shows that the war in the last half century has been fought to keep the own justice and safety of both sides of the conflict.

(2) In those countries who keep armed forces the supreme commander may give marching orders to them in accordance with the constitution as a justified action of collective defense right and so the people of those nations are dragged into a war without their intention.

The Japanese nationals who underwent the miserable experience through the Great East Asian War which aimed the Asian emancipation from the Occidental colonies created the Article 9 of the constitution which stipulated the renunciation of armed forces for the first time in world history.

As the results, the Japanese people who do not have the armed forces have never been engaged in any war for more than a past half century. At present, almost all the constitutions in the world stipulate the renunciation of the war of aggression but only two countries, i.e. Japan and Costa Rica have the constitution that stipulates the renunciation of armed forces. Those two countries have never been involved in the war for the past half century.

(3) When the Chinese invade Senkaku Islands, they will surely claim that they do so in order to protect their homeland against Japanese invasion. When the Japanese try to take back Takeshima, Shimane prefecture which Korea is occupying dispatching JSDF, the Korean armed forces will surely try to drive them back as an inevitable action of self-defense. Also, if Japan dispatches JSDF to take back Northern territories of Hokkaido from Russia, Russian armed forces will repel them as an action of self-defense.

Actually, every nation whose territories are occupied by other nations usually control themselves not using actual forces.

(4) If the Chinese PLA invade the Senkaku Islands, JSDF will surely protect the lands in accordance with JSDF law. The defense of homeland is not a constitutional matter but a administration matter. In the same manner, how to take back the northern territories or Takeshima Islands from Russia or Korea depends on the decision of the Japanese nationals and the actual action to be taken by the cabinet based on the will of the nationals, which is not decided by the constitution. In any way, the matter depends of the will of the people, i.e. the supreme national organ that is the Diet which comprises of the representatives of the people decides and the cabinet acts based on that decision.

17. "Self-Defense" is not a right given by others.

Q17.
The self-defense right is recognized by international laws, so should we not stipulate clearly the self-defense right in our constitution?

A17.
"Self-Defense" is a natural concept meaning an action which all living things or social organizations take to protect themselves from others' attack to continue their existence. Therefore, it is not a right to be provided to the people or the nation by any international law or constitution.

In other words, it is not that the nation and/or the people can defend themselves because the international laws and/or constitution admit that action, but the nation and/or the people defend themselves from the attack because otherwise they would become extinct.

Accordingly, it is quite natural that the Japanese constitution does not purposely stipulate the self-defense as a right of the nation to defend themselves from other's invasion. The fact that the Japanese keep their self-defense forces against a possible invasion from other nations does not contradict Article 9 of the constitution which stipulates the renunciation of war, right of belligerency and military forces.

The United Nations which was organized aiming the world peace established the collective security system to keep international peace, but for the practice of the system it is necessary to have the decision of the Security Council where the five victory nations keep the veto power. As this system is not feasible to settle the disputes, many powerful nations have continued to keep conventional military alliances. Therefore, the Article 51 of the UN Charter determined to admit such alliances as the action based on the collective defense right.

However, as Japan renounced the war as means of settling international disputes in Article 9 of the Constitution and as she does not have military forces, she has not been engaged in any military alliances with other country nor have executed the action of collective defense right based on Article 51 of the UN Charter.

Right now, the Abe Administration aims to revise Japan-US Security Treaty so as to be able to execute the so-called collective defense right in spite of the Article 9 of the Constitution and aims to revise JSDF law as well as the relative laws as early as possible.

Under the constitution which clearly determines the renunciation of military forces as well as the belligerent right of the nation whether the revised JSDF law can keep consistency with the constitution -----the people are watching carefully the development.

18. JSDF Defends the Nation

Q18.
　JSDF cannot yet take the major role in the security of our nation and we cannot rely on them fully for our security.　The main player in our defense is the US military forces and JSDF is only its complimentary. In such situation, Japan cannot be called an independent nation.　Should we not revise the Constitution to have the military forces in grand style?

A18.
It is the people of the nation themselves who defend the country and it is wrong for them to let other nation to defend their security.　If Japan faces the invasion from the forces of other country, JSDF immediately fight against them based on JSDF law but the US military forces may or may not participate in the fight in view of the then international politics although they are obliged to do so in accordance with the Japan-US Security Treaty.　(Like in case of Japan-USSR Nonaggression Pact the obligations in the international treaties have very often been denied in international history.　It is a matter of course that we should always do our best to foster friendly relations with the US so that such discrepancies will never happen.)

　Under the occupation of the Allied Forces after WWⅡ, it was true that the occupation forces played the role of Japanese security, but after the independence of Japan after the Peace Treaty with Allied Nations, such a situation could not continue.　First of all, the people of the US would not accept such situation anymore.
　Therefore, it was imperative and was natural that Japan at in 1950 created the National Police Reserve and as time developed, the Japan concluded the Japan-US Security Treaty with the US to secure more firmly her peace and safety. Thereafter the National Police Reserve (later changed into National Safety Forces in 1952) fortifying its strength with ex-soldiers of Imperial Forces helped

by the cooperation of American forces stationed in Japan and reached to become present JSDF.

Now how strong is the ability of present JSDF?
It is a very difficult task to compare fairly the ability of each nation's military power because there are innumerable variables to determine such ability like the numbers
of soldiers, airplanes, fleets, tanks, etc. plus the electronic apparatuses carried by such equipment, the numbers of artillery and weapons, etc., and the levels of the organization structure, the tactics, the strategy, the morale, the skill etc. Once in the Japanese Imperial Forces, it was commonly said that "By the strength of soldiers one soldier can fight favorably against a hundred of enemies.
You can never measure the force of each military strength like giving scores at an entrance exams of the universities.

In fact, the comparison of the military strength is the essential theme of the JSDF (the Joint Staff Council, ex-Joint Chiefs of Staff of the Imperial Forces) in an aim to foster and maintain the ability to defeat the possible enemy in all times.

Although it is a very difficult task for us to determine their strength, if you compare the amount of the military budget of each nation, we realize that JSDF is one of the top ten biggest establishment in the world.
But more important is how those military establishments as JSDF are receiving daily practice based on the well-studied strategic plan against the possible enemies. They are the professional of the war.

JSDF's aim is solely to defend the nation under Article 9 of the Constitution and has been grown up to a certain level through the history of more than a half century. However, it is another problem whether they can demonstrate their ability fully in the guerrilla warfare in Afghanistan or in the Middle East if Abe Cabinet abruptly throw them in the joint operation with USAF as a display of the collective defense right under the present Constitution.

JSDF headquarters who are directly responsible for the life of the whole troops now look to start the preparation for the possible movement of the government.

In November 2016, 350 JSDF members of the installation group of No.9 Division in Aomori was dispatched to South Sudan in Africa, after being trained for the so-called "new duty".

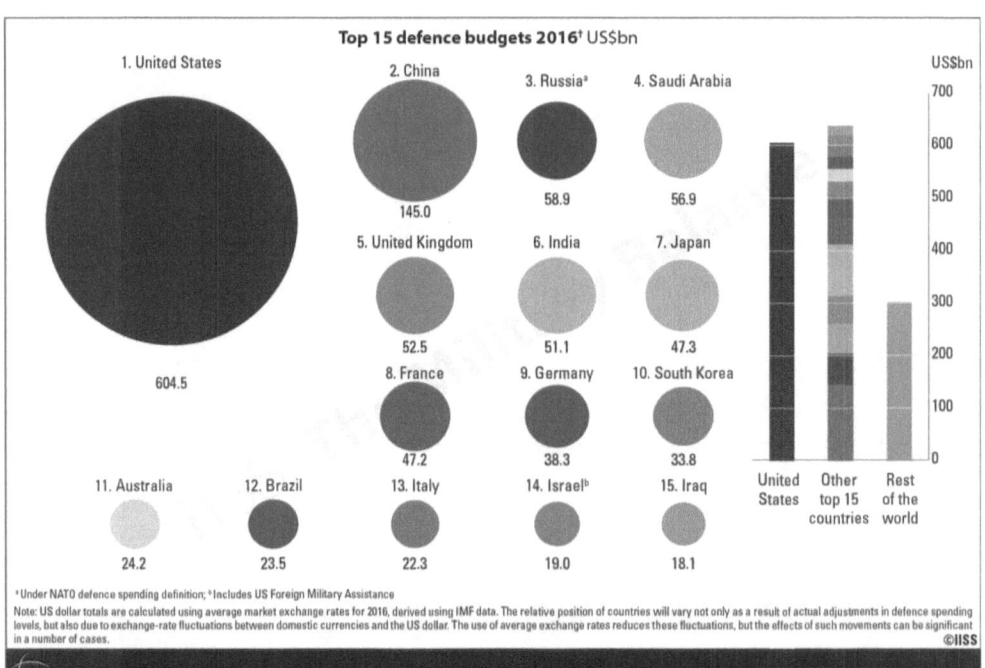

Top Ten Defense Budgets

US$bn

Nation	2016	1999
1. United States	604.5	283.1
2. China	145.0	39.9
3. Russia	58.9	56.8
4. Saudi Arabia	56.9	31.9

5. United Kingdom	52.5	36.9
6. India	51.1	15.0
7. Japan	47.3	40.4
8. France	47.2	37.9
9. Germany	38.3	31.1
10. South Korea	33.8	N.A.

Sorce: *The Military Balance 2017*: IISS(The International Institute for Strategic Studies http://www.iiss.org/-/media//images/publications/the%20military%20balance/milbal2016/mb%202016%20top%2015%20defence%20budgets%202015.jpg?la=en

As you see from the above, Japan was ranked 3rd in 1999, but was ranked 7th in 2016, doing justice to her position as the pacific country.

Moreover, JSDF, who have been gradually equipped with the latest spearheaded and high-tech weapons within the limit of the budget, have always been aiming to achieve the defense of the nation and have not kept any aggressive weapons to attack other nations nor have been engaged in the exercises of attacking other countries.   Please pay attention that all top eight nations except Saudi Arabia and Japan are nuclear-armed nations in the above list.

The nuclear weapons are of no use except for the purpose of explosion in other countries than the owner nation herself, and it's use does more harm than good to defend owner's homeland.   Although it is possible to make pressures to the enemy by keeping the nuclear weapons but once you use them you will have to expect the counter attack with the same nuclear weapons by the enemy.   On the top of it the nuclear effect will be extended widely in the geographical regions as well as in the long period of time, and thus will bring about fatal damages to the whole world.   It will ruin not only the belligerent nations but also the whole world.   Just for that reason, among the nuclear powers the negotiations are being seriously proceeded to achieve the reduction of those nuclear weapons.

10.5 ポ、43 字×34 行（四六判 43 字×17 行/頁の 2 頁分）

19. The renunciation of war is the common aspiration of the world

Q19.
The Philippines where I live also renounced the war in the constitutions with the words like those of the Japanese Constitution Article 9, influenced by the United States, and still keep the full-fledged armed forces.　I want to know more about the Costa Rican constitution which determines the renunciation of armed forces.

A19.
(1) We recall the serious damage suffered at the Leyte Island in November,2013, which is widely known as the site of a hard fought battle at the Great East Asian War.　Article 2 Section 2 of the Constitution of the Republic of the Philippines defines the renunciation of war in accordance with the international law.

Since 1928 antiwar pact (General Treaty for renunciation of War as an Instrument of National Policy = Kellogg-Briand Treaty), every nation expresses her position about the definition of war depending on the time and the situation. But it can be said that a war of aggression is supposed to be illegal in accordance with the generally agreed rule of international law.　The renunciation of aggressive war is determined in the constitutions of almost all the countries of the world.　The constitution of the Philippines is supposed to follow this world tendency.

However, it determines by the following Section 3 the superiority of the citizens over the military, thus admits the existence of the armed forces.　In Section 4 the government is determined to have duty to protect the security and protection of the nationals and the nationals are requested to join the armed forces or engage in the public duty as decided by the law.

Therefore, although the Philippines constitution defines the renunciation of war, it admits the power(government) to mobilize citizens to war by reasoning such action is necessary to keep national safety.

(2) Let us compare with Article9 of Japanese Constitution

In Section 1 of Article 9, it declares that the Japanese people forever renounce war as a sovereign right of the nation and the threat or use of force as means of settling international disputes. Under this clause, the power (the government is required to depend on solely peaceful negotiation (the negotiation without using force) for settling international disputes.

On the top of it, the Section 2 of the article 9 determined not to maintain "land, sea and air forces", which is a most simple expression that nobody can misunderstand the meaning, and moreover, to make it sure, the following sentence determined that the right of belligerency of the state will not be recognized.

When you compare the Japanese Constitution with the Philippine Constitution, you understand the former is such a forefront, deep devoted pacific constitution now existing in the world.

(3) Against this considerate terms of Article 9 of the Japanese Constitution, no power (government) has been able to act defying the purpose of the clause.

The fact that, for more than a past century, Japan has not been involved the wars that the US, her most friendly nation, are engaged in, proves the validity of this constitution.

(4) Today, only the Article 12 of the Constitution of Costa Rica (1949), which was established two years after Japanese constitution, determines the similar meaning to the Article 9 of the Japanese Constitution.

The Section 1 clearly determines the abolition of the Army. And Section 2 determines the police forces for surveillance and the preservation of public order, and a possible military organization for the national defense. This military force is supposed to be the similar organization of JSDF.

The territory space, the population, national circumstances of Costa Rica are different from those of Japan, and it is quite understandable that the terms of the article is just sufficient as it is. On the other hand, Japan, who fought to the last the Great East Asian War against surrounding big nations for four years and experienced the fatal attack of the nuclear bombs, must have worked out such minute sentences of the Article 9.

However, notwithstanding that such clear clauses are defined in the constitution, there are signs of denying the article with the excuse of using "collective defense right".

No matter how clear the sentences of the constitution are, the power(government) can move the society to what the believed to be, if the peoples' will to protect the constitution is fragile.

On July 1, 2014, the Second Abe Cabinet changed the conventional interpretation of the Article 9 after changing the top official of the Cabinet Legislation Bureau, so that the government can send abroad JSDF as an use of "collective defense right". The changes of the relative laws are being processed.

Treaty for the renunciation of war 1929 (Extract)===Kellogg–Briand Pact

ARTICLE I

The High Contracting Parties solemnly declare in the names of their respective peoples that they condemn recourse to war for the solution of international controversies, and renounce it, as an instrument of national policy in their relations with one another.

ARTICLE II

The High Contracting Parties agree that the settlement or solution of all disputes or conflicts of whatever nature or of whatever origin they may be, which may arise among them, shall never be sought except by pacific means.

戰爭抛棄ニ關スル條約（抜粋）
第一條　締約國ハ國際紛爭解決ノ爲戰爭ニ訴フルコトヲ非トシ且其ノ相互關係ニ於テ國家ノ政策ノ手段トシテノ戰爭ヲ抛棄スルコトヲ其ノ各自ノ人民ノ名ニ於テ嚴肅ニ宣言ス

第二條　締約國ハ相互間ニ起ルコトアルベキ一切ノ紛爭又ハ紛議ハ其ノ性質又ハ起因ノ如何ヲ問ハズ平和的手段ニ依ルノ外之ガ處理又ハ解決ヲ求メザルコトヲ約ス

フランス1946年憲法前文（抜粋）
　フランス共和国は、その伝統に忠実に従い、国際公法の諸規則を遵守する。フランス共和国は、征服を目的としたいかなる戦争も企てないし、その武力をいかなる国民に対しても決して使用しないであろう。フランスは、相互主義の留保のもとに、平和の組織と防衛に必要な主権制限に同意する。

フィリピン共和国憲法（1987年）（抜粋）
　第2条　フィリピンは、国策遂行の手段としての戦争を放棄し、一般に受諾された国際法の原則を国内法の一部として採用し、平和・平等・正義・自由・努力・すべての国の友好の政策を固く支持する。

コスタリカ共和国憲法(1949年)抜粋
　Artículo 12.- Se proscribe el Ejército como institución permanente. Para la vigilancia y conservación del orden público, habrá las fuerzas de policía necesarias. Sólo por convenio continental o para la defensa nacional podrán organizarse fuerzas militares; unas y otras estarán siempre subordinadas al poder civil; no podrán deliberar, ni hacer manifestaciones o declaraciones en forma individual o colectiva.（原文：スペイン語）

　ARTICLE 12. The Army as a permanent institution is abolished. There shall be the necessary police forces for surveillance and the preservation of public order. Military forces may only be organized under a continental agreement or for the national defence; in either case, they shall always be subordinate to the civil power: they may not deliberate or make statements or representations individually or collectively.（英訳文）

日本国憲法（抜粋）
第九条
1　日本国民は、正義と秩序を基調とする国際平和を誠実に希求し、国権の発動たる戦争と、武力による威嚇又は武力の行使は、国際紛争を解決する手段としては、永久にこれを放棄する。
2　前項の目的を達するため、陸海空軍その他の戦力は、これを保持しない。国の交戦権は、これを認めない。

20. Constitutional Reform Draft of LDP

Q20. What are the points of the LDP constitutional reform draft?

A20.
On April 27, 2012, the Liberal Democratic Party of Japan issued the draft of the constitutional reform.

The most important point the draft is that, aiming is to move from the sovereignty of the people to the constitutional monarchy, the Japanese people should have the unyielding spirit of protecting the nation from the first, and the flag of the Rising Sun and the "Kimigayo" are determined as the national flag and the national anthem by Article 3 of the constitution instead of the present Law of National Flag and National Anthem. Other important point is to change the present Self-Defense Force to National Defense Force by Article 9 so as to make it possible to dispatch the armed forces to overseas in order to protect the nation even when the country is not invaded.

The Constitution of the Empire of Japan (1889) defined the emperor as the head of the Empire, who exercises the rights of sovereignty, whereas the present Constitution of Japan determines that the Emperor shall be the symbol of the State and of the unity of the people, in accordance with the peoples' will which, on the one hand, strongly wishes the sovereignty to rest with the people, but on the other hand, wishes the continuity of the emperor whom many people love and respect.　　LDP draft aims to put emperor in the position like constitutional monarchy of other nations of the world

The laws that the nation establishes are to regulate the behavior of the people, whereas the constitution is to regulate the behavior of the governing power.　　In Japan, the laws that the Diet as the supreme organ of the nation establishes the laws by which the governing power freely regulates the behavior of the people, but those laws should not override the regulations of the constitution.

For that reason, as Japan renounces war as means of settling international disputes in Article 9 of the constitution, the government engages in the settlement of the territorial disputes such as the Senkaku, the Takeshima, and the northern territories as well as north Korean abduction problem only through diplomatic negotiations instead of the negotiation by force. Also, she will never dispatch forces to other countries like middle-east, Afghanistan, Pakistan, east Africa, etc. where her allied nation like US are engaged in war, even when US requests her to do so.

LDP constitutional reform draft aims to ease the regulation of Article 9 of the constitution upon the government so as to make it possible for the government to do such actions.

When this LDP draft was issued, the opinion poll showed that most the people welcomed the draft. I wonder how many Japanese people understood the real intention of the power.

Constitution of Japan (extract)

Chapter 2

RENUNCIATION OF WAR

Article 9.
1. Aspiring sincerely to an international peace based on justice and order, the Japanese people forever renounce war as a sovereign right of the nation and the threat or use of force as means of settling international disputes.
2. In order to accomplish the aim of the preceding paragraph, land, sea, and air forces, as well as other war potential, will never be maintained. The right of belligerency of the state will not be recognized.

Liberal Democratic Party

Draft for Reform of Japanese Constitution (Extract)
Chapter 2 National Security
Article 9 (Pacifism)
1. Aspiring sincerely to an international peace based on justice and order, the Japanese people forever renounce war as a sovereign right of the nation and do not use the threat or use of force as means of settling international disputes
2. The preceding paragraph does not deny the action of national defense right.

Article 9-2(National defense Force)
1. In order to secure national peace and independence as well as the security of the nation and the people, the National Defense Forces shall be maintained under the prime minister as the supreme commander.
2. The National Defense Forces shall fulfil the duty under the approval of the Diet and its control in accordance with the provisions of the relative law.
3. Apart from the duties as stipulated in Section 1, the National Defense Forces may engage in the activities in the international cooperation to secure peace and security of the international society as well as the activities to protect the life and freedom of the people in accordance with the provisions of the relative laws.
4. In addition to what are defined by the preceding 2 sections, the organization, the control and the matters related to the maintenance of secrecy shall be determined by the law.
5. In order to try the servicemen and other officials of the National Defense Forces who commit crimes in the course of fulfilling duties or who committed crimes relating to the maintenance of secrecy, a court of justice shall be established in the National Defense Forces.   In this case, the appealing right of the accused must be secured.

Article 9-3 (Territorial Securities)

   To protect the sovereignty and independence, the nation must preserve the territorial land, waters and airspace and secure the natural resources in cooperation with the people.

21. Originality of Japanese constitution

Q21 No nation in the world would like to open war willingly. When most countries in the world pledge to renounce war, what is the originality of Japanese constitution?

A21.
1. The point of Article 9 of the constitution lies in Section 2.

Section 1 is not the original of Japan as the similar expression has been taken into the constitution of many countries since almost all nations in the world agreed to renounce war as means of settling international disputes by the Treaty for the renunciation of war 1929 =Kellogg-Briand Pact=.

Section 2 declares the renunciation of armed forces by using such an easy expression as "In order to accomplish the aim of the preceding paragraph, land, sea, and air forces, as well as other war potential, will never be maintained," and moreover determines as " The right of belligerency of the state will not be recognized."   That is the unprecedented constitutional clause in the world, though two years later the constitution of the Republic of Costa Rica (1949) determined the similar clause in its Article 12.

Since WW2 the principal countries of the world have been dispatching their own armed forces to other countries on the premise that the action is not to invade but to defend the peace of the nation and the world.   But as its constitution is expressed by such clear sentences, the Japanese power (government) has been unable to establish armed forces and send the people to the war.

2. JSDF is not armed forces

JSDF is an organization established by law in accordance with the constitution in an aim to defend peace and independence of the nation when the nation is invaded. Not like armed forces which can be mobilized by the power (government) at any time when they judge it necessary to settle disputes, JSDF is solely to self-defend the nation, therefore it is not to threat other nations nor advance to foreign countries.

"Self-defense" is a concept of natural laws that any living creatures or social organizations protect themselves against the attacks from others, and it is not the "right" that is to be given by the international laws or the constitution.

In other words, the nations as well as the individuals are to protect themselves not because the international law or the constitution admits but because their existence should cease if they do not defend their safety. Therefore, it is easily understood that there is no stipulation in the Constitution of Japan that the nation has the self-defense right, which is quite clear and natural. The fact that the Japanese Diet established the JSDF law to defend the nation against any possible invasion from others does not contradict at all with the Article 9 of the constitution determining the renunciation of war, belligerency right and armed forces. Is there any countries in the world which put such a clause like "the nation can self-defend its country" to their constitution?

The United Nations established the collective security system in order to maintain world peace, but as the UN armed forces are to be formed only by the unanimous decision of the 5 permanent members of the Security Council, almost no such armed forces have ever been realized. Accordingly, most big powers have continued their military alliance to secure their own safety, and the Article 51 of the UN Charter admits such action to defend the nation with the individual military alliances under the notion of "collective defense right".

For more than a half century, Japan, who has no armed forces, has never sent JSDF abroad as an action in accordance with the use of collective defense right as stipulated in Article 51 of the UN Charter.

Right now Abe Cabinet is in the process of the constitutional reform so as to achieve the revival of the armed forces (national defense forces), revision of Japan-US Security Treaty to bilateral military treaty.

3. Dispatch of JSDF to South Sudan

On November 18,2016 Defense Minister Tomomi Inada issued an SDF action order to partially revise the SDF action order concerning the implementation of international peace cooperation activities in South Sudan. The action order prescribed the implementation of "kaketsuke-keigo", i.e. "coming to protection of individuals related to operations in response to urgent request".

Upon the order, some 350 personnel of Logistic Support of 9th Division of Aomori were sent to the remote site outside Japan starting from 20th of the same month, after being trained specially to meet the requirements of the new duty.

Before the independence of South Sudan, the conflict between the Sudanese government (Islam and Arabic) and the Sudan People's Liberation Army (Christian and African) lasted for decades. Allegedly, about two million people were sacrificed. In January 2005, the peace agreement was signed, and in March the United Nations Mission in Sudan(UNMS) was established to support the peace treaty. With the support of UNMS, based on the result of local referendum held in January 2011 which showed about 99% of the total of valid ballots endorsed the independence of the southern part of Sudan from Sudan, which was realized finally on July 9, 2011.

Meanwhile the United Nations Mission in the Republic of South Sudan (UNMISS) was organized aiming at establishing peace and safety as well as supporting in creating suitable environment for South Sudan's development.

The point is this "independence of South Sudan". Although the Sudanese government accepted the result of the local referendum, the newly-born Republic of South Sudan has not been in good relations with surrounding countries. Even in Sudan tenacious opposition against the new nation has been continuing. Moreover, in the new nation the political leaders are divided among themselves and fight each other.

　UNMISS is not the UN army as stipulated in Articles 39-50 but a so-called PKO (Peace Keeping Operations) , and so whether or not a member nation cooperate with UNMISS depend on each nation's policy.　Advanced UN nation members financially support the PKO at the same rate as ordinary share of the UN expenses.　Accordingly, in 2015, Japanese bear 10.833% of PKO expense which ranks 2nd following US share of 28.3626%. (MOFA HP)

　Regarding UNMISS, apart from the above financial support, Japan has dispatched staff officers since November 2011 and the engineering unit since January 2012.　But the recent dispatch of JSDF was on the supposition of possible occurrence of military battles for the first time.　The security situation near Juba(capital of South Sudan) is said to be becoming deteriorating although being more stable compared with other regions.

　JSDF is from the first not armed forces, so they are not to be dispatched to other nations when Japanese territory itself is not attacked, however, the power(government) had been dispatching the engineering unit to the regions outside of battlefield and to the task limited to the infrastructural work.　But this time using the new word "kaketukekeigo", the government sent JSDF unit voluntarily after training them for the possible fighting on the spot.

　To South Sudan, at present some 14 nations including India, Bangladesh, Ethiopia, China, etc. but no developed nations like US and EU nations participate in the activities except Japan and the UK, which is the ex-suzerain state.
　The arms and ammunition that both government and anti-government troop us are said to be mostly made in China or in Russia.　(At Syrian conflict, the most advanced arms of Russia and US are widely used.)

Sudan has the history for more than thousands of years comparable to Egypt and has been suffering the conflicts among many tribes, plus invasion from north like Egypt, France, the UK as well as the intervention from US, China, Russia with regards to natural resources make the political situation more complicated. It is really disappointing that on the top of those big nations such a peaceful country like Japan send "SDF" all the way from the far-east. Also, much sympathy goes to those JSDF personnel and their family who are ordered by the power (government, i.e. prime minister and defense minister) the mission which is not original.

On May 27, 2017, the last 40 out of 350 members of JSDF dispatched to South Sudan returned to Japan arriving at Aomori Airport at 11:20 AM. The JSDF UN Peace Keeping Operation(PKO) that lasted more than 5 years now ended without any loss of life. The most impressive was the smile of welcoming family.

Epilogue – In Search of World Eternal Peace

(1) Never ending battle of human society

Of all the history of the universe of 13.7 billion years, the earth after its birth of 4.6 billion years ago remained as a world of death up to 3.8 billion years ago when creatures appeared on the earth as bacteria-like mono cells.

After that, thanks to the energy regularly falling down from the sun, the creatures continued to develop and become diversified. The creatures have kept up with the change of environments and have survived by their own power on this planet. The earth has now changed from the world of death to the world of living.

The human being who appeared on the earth some five million years ago, changed their life more secured and safe through acting as a group, acquired the energy by using fire, invented language and letters, enabling to exchange knowledge and convey their will to their colleague, thus "the men who communicate" changed to be "the men who think".

The groups developed to be the orderly societies controlled by each leader and the quarrels among the individuals were settled inside the society, but instead, the struggles occurred among the societies relating to the living territories and the protection of the life of members of the societies. From about one thousand years ago various societies which developed and expanded in different places of the world began to quarrel violently with one another due to the tremendous advancement of transportation. The national state based on the territory and the nation became gradually formed and the quarrels among the individuals became to be larger scale of struggles, i.e. the battle among the nations.

In pre-modern society, the leader secured the loyalty of the people by letting them know the rules of administration beforehand, but for the past one thousand years the demand of the people to restrict the arbitrary decision of the ruler gradually became more and more increased and the modern nation with the constitution were born one after another.

In 19th century, backed by the development of scientific technology, modern countries prevailed the world existing together with other backward countries that failed to keep up with the times. In 20th century, the 1st World War was fought among those modern nations and tremendous number of people had to experience miserable lives.　On the reflection of such history, the nations discussed and organized the League of Nations, to which most countries of the world joined.　After then the Antiwar Pact was agreed.

However, 20years after WW1, the 2nd World War was broken out, which resulted in still more disastrous calamity to the people.　As the results, the United Nations was established. The UN aimed the world eternal peace organizing the Security Council as a central establishment for keeping peace consisting of 5 victorious nations as its standing committee members who hold the real power, as well as other establishments relating to economy, culture, science, etc.

The UN Charter determined that if a member country is invaded by other country, that country does not fight by itself but, instead, the UN Forces established by the leadership of the Security Council fight against the invader, and before the arrival of UN Forces the invaded nation is to defend the nation by itself.

But , for the past half century, no UN Forces have formed by the decision of the Security Council, and in the meantime wars in which any of the 5 victorious nations participated have occurred in various districts of the world, where many people have suffered the miserable damages.

Wars are never welcome by people. Now what is the reason why wars happen and how can we not let it happen again?　Many people argue and try not let it happen again.

(2) Can we avoid wars depending upon the power (ruler)?

The present international society is supposed to exist as an aggregate of the clear sovereign states which involve the people and the territory.

In an understanding that wars are caused by the conflicts of national interest, leading to the collision of forces, the world's power(ruler) tends to adjust the national interest through UN and other diplomatic activities and puts it a paramount mission for them to keep a balance of power among nations.

However, it is common in the international politics that the entangled conflict of national interest urges each nation to be prepared for the possible collision of forces and to exert the utmost efforts to keep military priority over the countries concerned.

Now from such a view of history (so-called "power-politics view of history") the Indo/Pakistani relations, the Israel/Arabic relations, the Japan/China relations, South/North Korean relations, and other major international relations are well explained but it is difficult to explain why people could not stop the following wars which the US are engaged in.

(President' names are in parentheses)
1950-63 Korean War (Harry S. Truman)
1965-75 Vietnamese War (John F. Kennedy, Lyndon Baines Johnson, Richard Nixon)
1983 Grenada Invasion (Ronald Reagan)
1988 Guatemala Air Raid (Ronald Reagan)
1989 Panama Invasion (George Bush)
1991 The Gulf War (George Bush)
1992-94 Somalian Civil War (George Bush)
1999 Sudan Factory Bombing (William Jefferson Clinton)
2001-   Anti-Terrorism War: Iraq, Afghanistan, Pakistan, Libya, Syria (George Bush, Jr., Barack Obama)

There are too many cases of this nature that brought miserable condition to the people like those happened in Kosovo (Servia), Croatia, East Timor, South Sudan, Libya, Tunisia, Syria, Egypt, Iraq, Afghanistan, etc. etc.

Many of those battles are fought caused by people's distrust of politics for not satisfying their straitened circumstances, that urges them to support the anti-governmental movements.

World has changed dramatically since 20th century, when the celebrated scholars of international politics like Hans Morgenthau (1904-80) or E.H. Carr (1892-1982) who analyzed correctly the international relations based on the so-called power politics.

In the field of media, from the television that became popularized quickly after the introduction of color broadcasting in mid-20th century to the internet that was brought into widespread use towards the end of the century the people's capacity of gathering information and publicizing their opinion has undergone a tremendous advance. The power (the rulers) cannot monopolize the important information anymore.

In the field of medicine, starting from the development of antibiotics, surprising progress of medical science has been overcoming various incurable diseases, and today even treatment for cancer is not exceptional.

In the field of scientific technology, robots are utilized daily as a matter of course; and space development, nanotechnology, AI (Artificial Intelligence), IoT (Internet of Things) ┈┈┈ all those development press us to change the ways of living and thinking.

On the other hand, environmental problem, energy and atomic-power problem, global warming, homosexuality and AIDS are the problems that emerged just for the past half century. Those are problems that needs to be solved for the human being to continue to exist.

A decade ago, to protect the nation at the risk of one's life was a matter of course.　But now that the next generation must cope with such various questions to continue to live, young people now feel slight different from what the past generation felt.　Today it is becoming more and more difficult for the power (ruler) to mobilize people for the reason of protecting the national interest.

Some Chinese people who think by their own brains and oppose to the Communist dictatorship, some middle-east people who think by their own brains and oppose to Islamic religious government, some US people who oppose to the traditional politicians sending soldiers to every nook and corner of the world with the flag of justice and freedom; that kind of people now express their opinion freely by internet and discuss and influence with each other.　This situation looks like going to change the international society from nationalism to humanitarianism.

(3) "Zum ewigen Frieden" by Immanuel Kant, and Art.9 of Japanese Constitution

The readers of this booklet now understand that the Article 9 of the Japanese Constitution not only determines the renunciation of War but also the renunciation of armed forces, which is epoch-making and has proved its effect for past 70 years of Japanese history of peace keeping.

A German philosopher of Konigsberg, East Prussia, Immanuel Kant (1724-1804) wrote on the fundamental principles of peace in his book "Zum ewigen Frieden" as follows :

"In time, all standing armed forces must be abolished completely. "

Because the standing armed forces are always prepared to go fighting and are threatening other nations to war.　Every nation competes with others for the increase of military budget and the armed forces finally go on the offensive first against others in order to relieve itself of a heavy financial burden to keep peace.

Hiring men to kill or be killed is the same as placing them in the hands of another (nation) as a mere machine or a tool, which is an act inconsistent with the rights of humanity.

That philosophy is embodied in the Constitution of Japan.

The Constitution of Japan

CHAPTER II

RENUNCIATION OF WAR

Article 9.
 Aspiring sincerely to an international peace based on justice and order, the Japanese people forever renounce war as a sovereign right of the nation and the threat or use of force as means of settling international disputes.
 In order to accomplish the aim of the preceding paragraph, land, sea, and air forces, as well as other war potential, will never be maintained. The right of belligerency of the state will not be recognized.

 Kant went on to say in the same book as follows:
 "The voluntary and periodic military training of citizens to secure themselves and their homeland against external aggression is a separate case, different from the abolition of standing military forces."

 This philosophy is exactly embodied in the formation of Japanese Self-Defense Forces Law. (Extract)

 Art. 3 (Duty of Self-Defense Forces)
 Self-Defense Forces are assigned mainly the task of defending our nation to secure peace and independence of our nation and maintain the security of the nation as well as the task of keeping the public order when necessary.

 The eternal peace that Immanuel Kant longed for towards the end of 18th century may be still unrealized in 21st century

However, Japan, keeping the three principles of "not to attack other nation", "not to participate in the war among other nations" and "to let the nation not to be attacked by other nations", has realized peace for the past 71 years.

If Japanese by holding these principles can continue to keep peace for another 29 years, Japan would become the true peaceful nation who realize peace of 100 years.

Immanuel Kant in the heaven would be astonished to find a small oriental nation like Japan should have achieved his philosophy for 100 years in such modern period as time runs easily 10 times more rapid than his age.

Afterword

At the plebiscite, it is expected that the people think over the true meaning of Article 9 of the Constitution and that they pass a fair judgement so as to maintain and make the peace of Japan perpetual

I sincerely hope that all who took up this booklet will cooperate for the bright future of this country and the world.

Please e-mail any comments on the contents of this book to the following address.

kpyk@ya2.so-net.ne.jp

Yasuya Kato

References and Bibliography

(in Japanese only)

Interpretation of Art.9
芦田　均　『新憲法解釈(1946年、ダイヤモンド社刊)』（書肆心水　2013年）
芦田　均　『制定の立場で見る日本国憲法入門』（書肆心水　2013年）
大石義雄　『日本国憲法逐条講義』（有信堂　1954年）
樋口陽一　『四訂　憲法入門』（勁草書房　2008年）
小嶋和司、大石　眞　『憲法概観{第7版}』（有斐閣双書　2011年）

Establishment of the Constitution of Japan
国立国会図書館　『日本国憲法の誕生　Birth of the Constitution of Japan』
　　　　　　　　http://www.ndl.go.jp/constitution/
憲法問題研究会編　『憲法読本(上)(下)』（岩波新書　1965年）
西　修　『図説　日本国憲法の誕生』（河出書房新社　2012年）
＜テレビ＞　NHK制作『日本国憲法誕生』（NHKテレビ　2007年）
　　　　　　　　https://www.youtube.com/watch?v=L4xiKi2pHLM
＜映画＞　大澤　豊　監督『日本の青空』（インディーズ　2007年）
　　　　　　　　https://www.youtube.com/watch?v=eO1DtOueucU&t=121s

Amendment of Art.9
安倍晋三　『美しい国へ』（文春新書　2006年）
山室信一　『憲法9条の思想水脈』（朝日新聞社　2007年）
小林直樹　『憲法第九条』（岩波新書　1982年）
今井　一　『「憲法九条」国民投票』（集英社　2003年）
長谷部恭男　『憲法とは何か』（岩波新書　2006年）
長谷部恭男編　大森正輔、柳澤協二、青井未帆、木村草太　『検証・安保法案　どこが憲法違反か』（有斐閣　2015年）
樋口陽一・小林　節　『「憲法改正」の真実』（集英社新書　2016年）
浦田一郎、前田哲男、半田　滋　『ハンドブック　集団的自衛権』（**岩波ブックレット　2013年**）
阪田雅裕　『集団的自衛権の行使はなぜ許されないのか』（岩波ブックレット　2013年）
半田　滋　『日本は戦争をするのか―集団的自衛権と自衛隊』（岩波新書　2014年）

齋藤貴男『戦争のできる国へー安倍政権の正体』(朝日新書 2014年)
井上達夫『憲法の涙』(毎日新聞出版 2016年)
木村草太『憲法の創造力』(NHK出版新書 2013年)
白井 聡『永続敗戦論 戦後日本の核心』(株式会社太田出版 2013年)
＜映画＞ John Junkerman 監督『日本国憲法 The Constitution of Japan』(シグロ 2005年)

National Defense

防衛省・自衛隊 (Ministry of Defense) HP http://www.mod.go.jp/
豊下楢彦『安保条約の成立 －吉田外交と天皇外交－』(岩波新書 1996年)
豊下楢彦『集団的自衛権とは何か』(岩波新書 2007年)
豊下楢彦、古関彰一『集団的自衛権と安全保障』(岩波新書 2014年)
奥平康彦、山口二郎『集団的自衛権の何が問題か』(岩波書店 2014年)
田岡良一『永世中立と日本の安全保障』(有斐閣 1950年)
高坂正堯『大国日本の世渡り学ー国際摩擦を考える』(PHP研究所 1990年)
高坂正堯『海洋国家日本の構想』(中央公論社 1965年)

Territorial Integrity

William B. Heflin『Diayou/Senkaku Islands Dispute: Japan and China, Ocean Apart』(Asian-Pacific Law & Policy Journal 2001年)1
松井芳郎『国際法学者がよむ尖閣問題』(日本評論社 2014年)
井上 清『尖閣列島ー釣魚諸島の史的解明』(第三書館 1996年)
池内 敏『竹島 － もうひとつの日韓関係史』(中公新書 2016年)
枝村純郎『外交交渉回想 －沖縄返還、福田ドクトリン・北方領土』(吉川弘文館 2016年)
若泉 敬『他策ナカリシヲ信ゼムト欲ス －核密約の真実－』(文藝春秋社 2009年)
佐藤栄作『佐藤栄作日記』(朝日新聞社 1997年)
劉暁波 野澤俊敬訳『現代中国知識人批判 (中国当代知識分子与政治)』(徳間書店 1992年)

War of Japan

朝日新聞法廷記者団『東京裁判(上)(中)(下)』(国土建設調査会出版局 1962年)
三根生久大『東京裁判(記録写真集)』(ダイナミックセラーズ出版 1998年)
林 三郎『太平洋戦争陸戦概史』(岩波新書 1956年)
麻田貞雄『両大戦間の日米関係-海軍と政策決定過程』(東京大学出版会 1994年)
ダグラス・マッカーサー 津島一夫訳『**マッカーサー大戦回顧録**』(中公新書 2014年)

佐藤　優『日米開戦の真実－大川周明著「米英東亜侵略史」(1941年)を読み解く』(小学館　2006年)

東條由布子『大東亜戦争の真実－東條英機宣誓供述書』(ワック(株)　2005年)
東條由布子『祖父東條英機「一切語るなかれ」増補改訂版』(文春文庫　2000年)
渡部昇一『東条英機歴史の証言-東京裁判宣誓供述書を読みとく』(祥伝社　2006年)
入江曜子『溥儀―清朝最後の皇帝』(岩波書店　2006年)
岡本幸治『北　一輝』(ミネルヴァ書房　2010年)
石原莞爾『最終戦争論』　(立命館出版部　1940年初版)(中公文庫　1993年)
榊山　潤『小説　石原莞爾』(元々社　1949年)
藤村安芸子『石原莞爾―愛と最終戦争』(講談社　2007年)
田中隆吉『敗因を衝く　軍閥専横の実相』(中公文庫　初刊山水社　1946年)
田中隆吉『日本軍閥暗闘史』(中公文庫　初刊静和堂書店　1948年)
西浦　進『昭和陸軍秘録』(日本経済新聞出版社　2014年)
北岡伸一『官僚制としての日本陸軍』(筑摩書房　2012年)
橋本衛ほか『硫黄島決戦』(光人社NF文庫　2007年)
秋草鶴次『十七歳の硫黄島』(文春新書　2006年)
柘植久慶『栗林忠道』(PHP文庫　2007年)
サンケイ新聞出版局『終戦への決断―証言記録太平洋戦争』(サンケイ新聞出版局　1975年)
John W. Dauer "EMBRACING DEFEAT – Japan in the wake of World War Ⅱ" (W.W. Norton 1999年)
E. H. Carr "International Relations between the Two World Wars 1919-1939"(Macmillan & Co 1955年)
H.J.Morgenthau『世界政治と国家理性』(創文社　1954年)鈴木成高・湯川宏訳)
半藤一利『昭和史 1926-1945』(㈱平凡社　2009年)
加藤陽子『満州事変から日中戦争へ』(岩波新書　2007年)
加藤陽子『それでも、日本人は「戦争」を選んだ』(新潮文庫　2016年)
岡　義武『全訂　近代ヨーロッパ政治史』(弘文堂　1956年)
田母神俊雄『日本は侵略国家であったのか』(ワックマガジンズ㈱　2009年)
中西輝政『**田母神論文の歴史的意義**』(ワックマガジンズ㈱　2009年)

National Polity of Japan
小島　毅『靖国史観　－　幕末維新という深淵』(ちくま新書　2007年)
赤澤史朗『靖国神社―せめぎあう＜戦没者追悼＞のゆくえ』(岩波書店　2005年)
福永武彦訳『古事記　上巻・中巻　下巻抄』(河出書房新社　1980年)
島崎　晋『らくらく読める　古事記』(広済堂出版　2003年)
津田左右吉『イサナギ・イサナミ二神が国土を生み成した物語』(岩波書店　1963年)

神野志隆光　大庭みな子『古事記・日本書紀　新潮古典文学アルバム』（新潮社　1991年）

Japanese Diplomacy

陸奥宗光『蹇蹇録』（岩波文庫　1983年）
幣原喜重郎『外交五十年』（読売新聞社　1951年）（中公文庫　2015年　改版発行）
重光　葵『昭和の動乱（上・下巻）』（中央公論社　1952年）
チャオ埴原三鈴・中馬清福『「排日移民法」と闘った外交官　―　1920年代日本外交と駐米全権大使・
　　　　埴谷正直』（（株）藤原書店　2011年）
田中　均『外交の力』（日本経済新聞出版社　2009年）

Reality of Modern Wars

Lawrence Wright　平賀秀明訳『倒壊する巨塔　The Looming Tower（上）（下）』（白水社　2009年）
Max Weber　脇　圭平　訳『職業としての政治　POLITIK ALS BERUF 1919』（岩波文庫　1991年））
内藤正典『トルコ　中東情勢のカギをにぎる国』（集英社　2016年）
山内昌之『中東複合危機から第三次世界大戦へ　―　イスラームの悲劇』（PHP新書　2016年）
Robert Kagan　山岡洋一訳『ネオコンの論理　Of Paradise and Power』（光文社　2003年）
川上和久『イラク戦争と情報操作』（宝島社　2004年）
川上和久『北朝鮮報道―情報操作を見抜く』（光文社　2004年）
Norbert Vollertsen　平野郷子訳『Diary of a Mad Place 北朝鮮を知りすぎた医師』（草思社　2003年）
李登輝『台湾の主張』（PHP研究所　1999年）
岡本幸治『インド世界を読む』（創成社新書　2006年）
鈴木紘司『イスラムのことがまんがで3時間でわかる本』（明日香出版社　2008年）
鈴木紘司『中東のことがまんがで3時間でわかる本』（明日香出版社　2008年）
Glenn Greenwald　田口俊樹ほか訳『暴露　スノーデンが私に託したファイル』（新潮社　2014年）
Stephen Pelletiere、荒井雅子訳『アメリカの石油戦争 America's Oil War』（ビジネス社　2006年）
Alex Goldfarb with Marina Litvinenko『リトビネンコ暗殺　Death of a Dissident』（早川書房　2007年）
Thomas B. Allen　佐藤正和訳『機密指定解除―歴史を変えた極秘文書 DECLASSIFIED 50 Top-
　　　　Secret Documents That Changed History』（日経ナショナルジオグラフィック社　2008年）
＜映画＞BLACK HAWK DOWN　（コロンビア映画　2002年）
＜映画＞A FEW GOOD MEN　（コロンビア映画　Tom Cruise、Jack Nicholson主演 1993年）
＜映画＞The Hurt Locker　（監督：Kathryn Bigelow　2008年）
＜映画＞Body of Lies　（主演：Leonardo Di Caprio　2009年）

War and Peace

Immanuel Kant　池内　紀　訳『永遠平和のために　Zum ewigen Frieden』（集英社　2015 年）

山口周三『南原繁の生涯　—　信仰・思想・業績』（教文館　2012 年）

田中明彦『新しい「中世」 21 世紀の世界システム』（日本経済新聞社　1996 年）

William J. Perry　春原　剛　訳『核なき世界を求めて In Search of No Nuclear World』（日本経済新聞
　　　　　　出版社　2011 年）

青木　理『日本会議の正体』（平凡社新書　2016 年）

矢野絢也『黒い手帖　創価学会「日本占領計画」の全記録』（講談社　2009 年）

佐藤　信『60 年代のリアル』（ミネルヴァ書房　2011 年）

半藤一利『昭和史　戦後篇　1945-1989』（㈱平凡社　2009 年）

渡辺利夫『新　脱亜論』（㈱文芸春秋　2008 年）

木村利人『戦争・平和・いのちを考える』（キリスト教新聞社　2016 年）

THE CONSTITUTION OF JAPAN

We, the Japanese people, acting through our duly elected representatives in the National Diet, determined that we shall secure for ourselves and our posterity the fruits of peaceful cooperation with all nations and the blessings of liberty throughout this land, and resolved that never again shall we be visited with the horrors of war through the action of government, do proclaim that sovereign power resides with the people and do firmly establish this Constitution. Government is a sacred trust of the people, the authority for which is derived from the people, the powers of which are exercised by the representatives of the people, and the benefits of which are enjoyed by the people. This is a universal principle of mankind upon which this Constitution is founded. We reject and revoke all constitutions, laws, ordinances, and rescripts in conflict herewith. We, the Japanese people, desire peace for all time and are deeply conscious of the high ideals controlling human relationship, and we have determined to preserve our security and existence, trusting in the justice and faith of the peace-loving peoples of the world. We desire to occupy an honored place in an international society striving for the preservation of peace, and the banishment of tyranny and slavery, oppression and intolerance for all time from the earth. We recognize that all peoples of the world have the right to live in peace, free from fear and want.

We believe that no nation is responsible to itself alone, but that laws of political morality are universal; and that obedience to such laws is incumbent upon all nations who would sustain their own sovereignty and justify their sovereign relationship with other nations.

We, the Japanese people, pledge our national honor to accomplish these high ideals and purposes with all our resources.

CHAPTER I

THE EMPEROR

Article 1. The Emperor shall be the symbol of the State and of the unity of the People, deriving his position from the will of the people with whom resides sovereign power.

Article 2. The Imperial Throne shall be dynastic and succeeded to in accordance with the Imperial House Law passed by the Diet.

Article 3. The advice and approval of the Cabinet shall be required for all acts of the Emperor in matters of state, and the Cabinet shall be responsible therefor.

Article 4. The Emperor shall perform only such acts in matters of state as are provided for in this Constitution and he shall not have powers related to government.
The Emperor may delegate the performance of his acts in matters of state as may be provided by law.

Article 5. When, in accordance with the Imperial House Law, a Regency is established, the Regent shall perform his acts in matters of state in the Emperor's name. In this case, paragraph one of the preceding article will be applicable.

Article 6. The Emperor shall appoint the Prime Minister as designated by the Diet.
The Emperor shall appoint the Chief Judge of the Supreme Court as designated by the Cabinet.

Article 7. The Emperor, with the advice and approval of the Cabinet, shall perform the following acts in matters of state on behalf of the people:

Promulgation of amendments of the constitution, laws, cabinet orders and treaties.
Convocation of the Diet.
Dissolution of the House of Representatives.
Proclamation of general election of members of the Diet.
Attestation of the appointment and dismissal of Ministers of State and other officials as provided for by law, and of full powers and credentials of Ambassadors and Ministers.

Attestation of general and special amnesty, commutation of punishment, reprieve, and restoration of rights.

Awarding of honors.

Attestation of instruments of ratification and other diplomatic documents as provided for by law.

Receiving foreign ambassadors and ministers.

Performance of ceremonial functions.

Article 8. No property can be given to, or received by, the Imperial House, nor can any gifts be made therefrom, without the authorization of the Diet.

CHAPTER II

RENUNCIATION OF WAR

Article 9. Aspiring sincerely to an international peace based on justice and order, the Japanese people forever renounce war as a sovereign right of the nation and the threat or use of force as means of settling international disputes.

In order to accomplish the aim of the preceding paragraph, land, sea, and air forces, as well as other war potential, will never be maintained. The right of belligerency of the state will not be recognized.

CHAPTER III

RIGHTS AND DUTIES OF THE PEOPLE

Article 10. The conditions necessary for being a Japanese national shall be determined by law.

Article 11. The people shall not be prevented from enjoying any of the fundamental human rights. These fundamental human rights guaranteed to the people by this Constitution shall be conferred upon the people of this and future generations as eternal and inviolate rights.

Article 12. The freedoms and rights guaranteed to the people by this Constitution shall be maintained by the constant endeavor of the people, who shall refrain from any abuse of these freedoms and rights and shall always be responsible for utilizing them for the public welfare.

Article 13. All of the people shall be respected as individuals. Their right to life, liberty, and the pursuit of happiness shall, to the extent that it does not interfere with the public welfare, be the supreme consideration in legislation and in other governmental affairs.

Article 14. All of the people are equal under the law and there shall be no discrimination in political, economic or social relations because of race, creed, sex, social status or family origin.
Peers and peerage shall not be recognized.
No privilege shall accompany any award of honor, decoration or any distinction, nor shall any such award be valid beyond the lifetime of the individual who now holds or hereafter may receive it.

Article 15. The people have the inalienable right to choose their public officials and to dismiss them.
All public officials are servants of the whole community and not of any group thereof.
Universal adult suffrage is guaranteed with regard to the election of public officials.
In all elections, secrecy of the ballot shall not be violated. A voter shall not be answerable, publicly or privately, for the choice he has made.

Article 16. Every person shall have the right of peaceful petition for the redress of damage, for the removal of public officials, for the enactment, repeal or amendment of laws, ordinances or regulations and for other matters; nor shall any person be in any way discriminated against for sponsoring such a petition.

Article 17. Every person may sue for redress as provided by law from the State or a public entity, in case he has suffered damage through illegal act of any public official.

Article 18. No person shall be held in bondage of any kind. Involuntary servitude, except as punishment for crime, is prohibited.

Article 19. Freedom of thought and conscience shall not be violated.

Article 20. Freedom of religion is guaranteed to all. No religious organization shall receive any privileges from the State, nor exercise any political authority. No person shall be compelled to take part in any religious act, celebration, rite or practice.
The State and its organs shall refrain from religious education or any other religious activity.

Article 21. Freedom of assembly and association as well as speech, press and all other forms of expression are guaranteed.
No censorship shall be maintained, nor shall the secrecy of any means of communication be violated.

Article 22. Every person shall have freedom to choose and change his residence and to choose his occupation to the extent that it does not interfere with the public welfare.
Freedom of all persons to move to a foreign country and to divest themselves of their nationality shall be inviolate.

Article 23. Academic freedom is guaranteed.

Article 24. Marriage shall be based only on the mutual consent of both sexes and it shall be maintained through mutual cooperation with the equal rights of husband and wife as a basis.
With regard to choice of spouse, property rights, inheritance, choice of domicile, divorce and other matters pertaining to marriage and the family, laws shall be enacted from the standpoint of individual dignity and the essential equality of the sexes.

Article 25. All people shall have the right to maintain the minimum standards of wholesome and cultured living.

In all spheres of life, the State shall use its endeavors for the promotion and extension of social welfare and security, and of public health.

Article 26. All people shall have the right to receive an equal education correspondent to their ability, as provided by law.
All people shall be obligated to have all boys and girls under their protection receive ordinary education as provided for by law. Such compulsory education shall be free.

Article 27. All people shall have the right and the obligation to work.
Standards for wages, hours, rest and other working conditions shall be fixed by law.
Children shall not be exploited.

Article 28. The right of workers to organize and to bargain and act collectively is guaranteed.

Article 29. The right to own or to hold property is inviolable.
Property rights shall be defined by law, in conformity with the public welfare.
Private property may be taken for public use upon just compensation therefor.

Article 30. The people shall be liable to taxation as provided by law.

Article 31. No person shall be deprived of life or liberty, nor shall any other criminal penalty be imposed, except according to procedure established by law.

Article 32. No person shall be denied the right of access to the courts.

Article 33. No person shall be apprehended except upon warrant issued by a competent judicial officer which specifies the offense with which the person is charged, unless he is apprehended, the offense being committed.

Article 34. No person shall be arrested or detained without being at once informed of the charges against him or without the immediate privilege of counsel; nor shall he be detained without adequate cause; and upon demand of any person such cause must be immediately shown in open court in his presence and the presence of his counsel.

Article 35. The right of all persons to be secure in their homes, papers and effects against entries, searches and seizures shall not be impaired except upon warrant issued for adequate cause and particularly describing the place to be searched and things to be seized, or except as provided by Article 33.
Each search or seizure shall be made upon separate warrant issued by a competent judicial officer.

Article 36. The infliction of torture by any public officer and cruel punishments are absolutely forbidden.

Article 37. In all criminal cases the accused shall enjoy the right to a speedy and public trial by an impartial tribunal.
He shall be permitted full opportunity to examine all witnesses, and he shall have the right of compulsory process for obtaining witnesses on his behalf at public expense.
At all times the accused shall have the assistance of competent counsel who shall, if the accused is unable to secure the same by his own efforts, be assigned to his use by the State.

Article 38. No person shall be compelled to testify against himself.
Confession made under compulsion, torture or threat, or after prolonged arrest or detention shall not be admitted in evidence.
No person shall be convicted or punished in cases where the only proof against him is his own confession.

Article 39. No person shall be held criminally liable for an act which was lawful at the time it was committed, or of which he has been acquitted, nor shall he be placed in double jeopardy.

Article 40. Any person, in case he is acquitted after he has been arrested or detained, may sue the State for redress as provided by law.

CHAPTER IV

THE DIET

Article 41. The Diet shall be the highest organ of state power, and shall be the sole law-making organ of the State.

Article 42. The Diet shall consist of two Houses, namely the House of Representatives and the House of Councillors.

Article 43. Both Houses shall consist of elected members, representative of all the people.
The number of the members of each House shall be fixed by law.

Article 44. The qualifications of members of both Houses and their electors shall be fixed by law. However, there shall be no discrimination because of race, creed, sex, social status, family origin, education, property or income.

Article 45. The term of office of members of the House of Representatives shall be four years. However, the term shall be terminated before the full term is up in case the House of Representatives is dissolved.

Article 46. The term of office of members of the House of Councillors shall be six years, and election for half the members shall take place every three years.

Article 47. Electoral districts, method of voting and other matters pertaining to the method of election of members of both Houses shall be fixed by law.

Article 48. No person shall be permitted to be a member of both Houses simultaneously.

Article 49. Members of both Houses shall receive appropriate annual payment from the national treasury in accordance with law.

Article 50. Except in cases provided by law, members of both Houses shall be exempt from apprehension while the Diet is in session, and any members apprehended before the opening of the session shall be freed during the term of the session upon demand of the House.

Article 51. Members of both Houses shall not be held liable outside the House for speeches, debates or votes cast inside the House.

Article 52. An ordinary session of the Diet shall be convoked once per year.

Article 53. The Cabinet may determine to convoke extraordinary sessions of the Diet. When a quarter or more of the total members of either House makes the demand, the Cabinet must determine on such convocation.

Article 54. When the House of Representatives is dissolved, there must be a general election of members of the House of Representatives within forty (40) days from the date of dissolution, and the Diet must be convoked within thirty (30) days from the date of the election.
When the House of Representatives is dissolved, the House of Councillors is closed at the same time. However, the Cabinet may in time of national emergency convoke the House of Councillors in emergency session.
Measures taken at such session as mentioned in the proviso of the preceding paragraph shall be provisional and shall become null and void unless agreed to by the House of Representatives within a period of ten (10) days after the opening of the next session of the Diet.

Article 55. Each House shall judge disputes related to qualifications of its members. However, in order to deny a seat to any member, it is necessary to pass a resolution by a majority of two-thirds or more of the members present.

Article 56. Business cannot be transacted in either House unless one-third or more of total membership is present.
All matters shall be decided, in each House, by a majority of those present, except as elsewhere provided in the Constitution, and in case of a tie, the presiding officer shall decide the issue.

Article 57. Deliberation in each House shall be public. However, a secret meeting may be held where a majority of two-thirds or more of those members present passes a resolution therefor.
Each House shall keep a record of proceedings. This record shall be published

and given general circulation, excepting such parts of proceedings of secret session as may be deemed to require secrecy.

Upon demand of one-fifth or more of the members present, votes of the members on any matter shall be recorded in the minutes.

Article 58. Each House shall select its own president and other officials.

Each House shall establish its rules pertaining to meetings, proceedings and internal discipline, and may punish members for disorderly conduct. However, in order to expel a member, a majority of two-thirds or more of those members present must pass a resolution thereon.

Article 59. A bill becomes a law on passage by both Houses, except as otherwise provided by the Constitution.

A bill which is passed by the House of Representatives, and upon which the House of Councillors makes a decision different from that of the House of Representatives, becomes a law when passed a second time by the House of Representatives by a majority of two-thirds or more of the members present.

The provision of the preceding paragraph does not preclude the House of Representatives from calling for the meeting of a joint committee of both Houses, provided for by law.

Failure by the House of Councillors to take final action within sixty (60) days after receipt of a bill passed by the House of Representatives, time in recess excepted, may be determined by the House of Representatives to constitute a rejection of the said bill by the House of Councillors.

Article 60. The budget must first be submitted to the House of Representatives.

Upon consideration of the budget, when the House of Councillors makes a decision different from that of the House of Representatives, and when no agreement can be reached even through a joint committee of both Houses, provided for by law, or in the case of failure by the House of Councillors to take final action within thirty (30) days, the period of recess excluded, after the receipt of the budget passed by the House of Representatives, the decision of the House of Representatives shall be the decision of the Diet.

Article 61. The second paragraph of the preceding article applies also to the Diet approval required for the conclusion of treaties.

Article 62. Each House may conduct investigations in relation to government, and may demand the presence and testimony of witnesses, and the production of records.

Article 63. The Prime Minister and other Ministers of State may, at any time, appear in either House for the purpose of speaking on bills, regardless of whether they are members of the House or not. They must appear when their presence is required in order to give answers or explanations.

Article 64. The Diet shall set up an impeachment court from among the members of both Houses for the purpose of trying those judges against whom removal proceedings have been instituted.
Matters relating to impeachment shall be provided by law.

CHAPTER V

THE CABINET

Article 65. Executive power shall be vested in the Cabinet.

Article 66. The Cabinet shall consist of the Prime Minister, who shall be its head, and other Ministers of State, as provided for by law.
The Prime Minister and other Ministers of State must be civilians.
The Cabinet, in the exercise of executive power, shall be collectively responsible to the Diet.

Article 67. The Prime Minister shall be designated from among the members of the Diet by a resolution of the Diet. This designation shall precede all other business.
If the House of Representatives and the House of Councillors disagree and if no agreement can be reached even through a joint committee of both Houses, provided for by law, or the House of Councillors fails to make designation within ten (10) days, exclusive of the period of recess, after the House of Representatives

has made designation, the decision of the House of Representatives shall be the decision of the Diet.

Article 68. The Prime Minister shall appoint the Ministers of State. However, a majority of their number must be chosen from among the members of the Diet. The Prime Minister may remove the Ministers of State as he chooses.

Article 69. If the House of Representatives passes a non-confidence resolution, or rejects a confidence resolution, the Cabinet shall resign en masse, unless the House of Representatives is dissolved within ten (10) days.

Article 70. When there is a vacancy in the post of Prime Minister, or upon the first convocation of the Diet after a general election of members of the House of Representatives, the Cabinet shall resign en masse.

Article 71. In the cases mentioned in the two preceding articles, the Cabinet shall continue its functions until the time when a new Prime Minister is appointed.

Article 72. The Prime Minister, representing the Cabinet, submits bills, reports on general national affairs and foreign relations to the Diet and exercises control and supervision over various administrative branches.

Article 73. The Cabinet, in addition to other general administrative functions, shall perform the following functions:
Administer the law faithfully; conduct affairs of state.
Manage foreign affairs.
Conclude treaties. However, it shall obtain prior or, depending on circumstances, subsequent approval of the Diet.
Administer the civil service, in accordance with standards established by law.
Prepare the budget, and present it to the Diet.
Enact cabinet orders in order to execute the provisions of this Constitution and of the law. However, it cannot include penal provisions in such cabinet orders unless authorized by such law.
Decide on general amnesty, special amnesty, commutation of punishment, reprieve, and restoration of rights.

Article 74. All laws and cabinet orders shall be signed by the competent Minister of State and countersigned by the Prime Minister.

Article 75. The Ministers of State, during their tenure of office, shall not be subject to legal action without the consent of the Prime Minister. However, the right to take that action is not impaired hereby.

CHAPTER VI

JUDICIARY

Article 76. The whole judicial power is vested in a Supreme Court and in such inferior courts as are established by law.
No extraordinary tribunal shall be established, nor shall any organ or agency of the Executive be given final judicial power.
All judges shall be independent in the exercise of their conscience and shall be bound only by this Constitution and the laws.

Article 77. The Supreme Court is vested with the rule-making power under which it determines the rules of procedure and of practice, and of matters relating to attorneys, the internal discipline of the courts and the administration of judicial affairs.
Public procurators shall be subject to the rule-making power of the Supreme Court.
The Supreme Court may delegate the power to make rules for inferior courts to such courts.

Article 78. Judges shall not be removed except by public impeachment unless judicially declared mentally or physically incompetent to perform official duties. No disciplinary action against judges shall be administered by any executive organ or agency.

Article 79. The Supreme Court shall consist of a Chief Judge and such number of judges as may be determined by law; all such judges excepting the Chief Judge shall be appointed by the Cabinet.

The appointment of the judges of the Supreme Court shall be reviewed by the people at the first general election of members of the House of Representatives following their appointment, and shall be reviewed again at the first general election of members of the House of Representatives after a lapse of ten (10) years, and in the same manner thereafter.

In cases mentioned in the foregoing paragraph, when the majority of the voters favors the dismissal of a judge, he shall be dismissed.

Matters pertaining to review shall be prescribed by law.

The judges of the Supreme Court shall be retired upon the attainment of the age as fixed by law.

All such judges shall receive, at regular stated intervals, adequate compensation which shall not be decreased during their terms of office.

Article 80. The judges of the inferior courts shall be appointed by the Cabinet from a list of persons nominated by the Supreme Court. All such judges shall hold office for a term of ten (10) years with privilege of reappointment, provided that they shall be retired upon the attainment of the age as fixed by law.

The judges of the inferior courts shall receive, at regular stated intervals, adequate compensation which shall not be decreased during their terms of office.

Article 81. The Supreme Court is the court of last resort with power to determine the constitutionality of any law, order, regulation or official act.

Article 82. Trials shall be conducted and judgment declared publicly.

Where a court unanimously determines publicity to be dangerous to public order or morals, a trial may be conducted privately, but trials of political offenses, offenses involving the press or cases wherein the rights of people as guaranteed in Chapter III of this Constitution are in question shall always be conducted publicly.

CHAPTER VII

FINANCE

Article 83. The power to administer national finances shall be exercised as the Diet shall determine.

Article 84. No new taxes shall be imposed or existing ones modified except by law or under such conditions as law may prescribe.

Article 85. No money shall be expended, nor shall the State obligate itself, except as authorized by the Diet.

Article 86. The Cabinet shall prepare and submit to the Diet for its consideration and decision a budget for each fiscal year.

Article 87. In order to provide for unforeseen deficiencies in the budget, a reserve fund may be authorized by the Diet to be expended upon the responsibility of the Cabinet.
The Cabinet must get subsequent approval of the Diet for all payments from the reserve fund.

Article 88. All property of the Imperial Household shall belong to the State. All expenses of the Imperial Household shall be appropriated by the Diet in the budget.

Article 89. No public money or other property shall be expended or appropriated for the use, benefit or maintenance of any religious institution or association, or for any charitable, educational or benevolent enterprises not under the control of public authority.

Article 90. Final accounts of the expenditures and revenues of the State shall be audited annually by a Board of Audit and submitted by the Cabinet to the Diet, together with the statement of audit, during the fiscal year immediately following the period covered.
The organization and competency of the Board of Audit shall be determined by law.

Article 91. At regular intervals and at least annually the Cabinet shall report to the Diet and the people on the state of national finances.

CHAPTER VIII

LOCAL SELF-GOVERNMENT

Article 92. Regulations concerning organization and operations of local public entities shall be fixed by law in accordance with the principle of local autonomy.

Article 93. The local public entities shall establish assemblies as their deliberative organs, in accordance with law.
The chief executive officers of all local public entities, the members of their assemblies, and such other local officials as may be determined by law shall be elected by direct popular vote within their several communities.

Article 94. Local public entities shall have the right to manage their property, affairs and administration and to enact their own regulations within law.

Article 95. A special law, applicable only to one local public entity, cannot be enacted by the Diet without the consent of the majority of the voters of the local public entity concerned, obtained in accordance with law.

CHAPTER IX

AMENDMENTS

Article 96. Amendments to this Constitution shall be initiated by the Diet, through a concurring vote of two-thirds or more of all the members of each House and shall thereupon be submitted to the people for ratification, which shall require the affirmative vote of a majority of all votes cast thereon, at a special referendum or at such election as the Diet shall specify.
Amendments when so ratified shall immediately be promulgated by the Emperor in the name of the people, as an integral part of this Constitution.

CHAPTER X

SUPREME LAW

Article 97. The fundamental human rights by this Constitution guaranteed to the people of Japan are fruits of the age-old struggle of man to be free; they have survived the many exacting tests for durability and are conferred upon this and future generations in trust, to be held for all time inviolate.

Article 98. This Constitution shall be the supreme law of the nation and no law, ordinance, imperial rescript or other act of government, or part thereof, contrary to the provisions hereof, shall have legal force or validity.
The treaties concluded by Japan and established laws of nations shall be faithfully observed.

Article 99. The Emperor or the Regent as well as Ministers of State, members of the Diet, judges, and all other public officials have the obligation to respect and uphold this Constitution.

CHAPTER XI

SUPPLEMENTARY PROVISIONS

Article 100. This Constitution shall be enforced as from the day when the period of six months will have elapsed counting from the day of its promulgation.
The enactment of laws necessary for the enforcement of this Constitution, the election of members of the House of Councillors and the procedure for the convocation of the Diet and other preparatory procedures necessary for the enforcement of this Constitution may be executed before the day prescribed in the preceding paragraph.

Article 101. If the House of Councillors is not constituted before the effective date of this Constitution, the House of Representatives shall function as the Diet until such time as the House of Councillors shall be constituted.

Article 102. The term of office for half the members of the House of Councillors serving in the first term under this Constitution shall be three years. Members falling under this category shall be determined in accordance with law.

Article 103. The Ministers of State, members of the House of Representatives and judges in office on the effective date of this Constitution, and all other public officials who occupy positions corresponding to such positions as are recognized by this Constitution shall not forfeit their positions automatically on account of the enforcement of this Constitution unless otherwise specified by law. When, however, successors are elected or appointed under the provisions of this Constitution, they shall forfeit their positions as a matter of course.

www.ingramcontent.com/pod-product-compliance
Lightning Source LLC
Chambersburg PA
CBHW030844180526
45163CB00004B/1440